BEGINNER'S
GARDEN

BEGINNER'S
GARDEN

A Practical Guide to Growing Vegetables & Fruit
without Getting Your Hands Too Dirty

Alex Mitchell

IMM **lifestyle**
◌**books**™

Read. Learn. Do What You Love.

Published 2018—IMM Lifestyle Books
www.IMMLifestyleBooks.com

IMM Lifestyle Books are distributed in the UK by
Grantham Book Service, Trent Road, Grantham,
Lincolnshire, NG31 7XQ.

In North America, IMM Lifestyle Books are distributed
by Fox Chapel Publishing, 903 Square Street, Mount
Joy, PA 17552, www.FoxChapelPublishing.com.

ISBN 978-1-5048-0098-3

Library of Congress Cataloging-in-Publication Data

Names: Mitchell, Alex, 1971– author.
Title: Beginner's garden / Alex Mitchell.
Description: Mount Joy, PA : IMM Lifestyle Books,
   2018. | "This book is an updated and revised version
   of The Girl's Guide to Growing Your Own, published
   2009 by New Holland Publishers (UK) Ltd." |
   Includes index.
Identifiers: LCCN 2017053416 | ISBN 9781504800983
   (pbk.)
Subjects: LCSH: Gardening. | Fruit. | Vegetables.
Classification: LCC SB450.97 .M56 2018 | DDC
   635—dc23
LC record available at https://lccn.loc.gov/2017053416

We are always looking for talented authors. To submit
an idea, please send a brief inquiry to
acquisitions@foxchapelpublishing.com.

Printed in Singapore
10 9 8 7 6 5 4 3 2 1

Contents

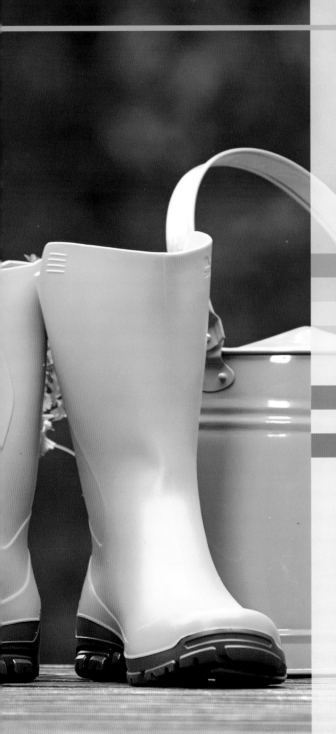

Preface to the Second Edition   6

Introduction   8

Getting Started   10

SPRING   32

SUMMER   74

Entertaining   110

AUTUMN   122

WINTER   138

Garden Villains   148

Glossary   153

Index   155

Resources   157

Acknowledgments   158

Photo Credits   158

About the Author   160

Preface to the Second Edition

WHEN I FIRST WROTE THIS BOOK, I had a tiny London garden, demanding toddlers, and an obsession for growing fruit and vegetables that was only slightly curtailed by the needs of the screaming toddlers and my own overambitiousness. In the 10 years since, during which my children have become less interested in my attention than that of their computer screens, I have swapped city life for a large rural garden, where the veg plot shares space with seven sheep, four chickens, and an apple orchard (currently being eaten by the seven sheep). But my love and fascination for growing fruit and vegetables has, if anything, become stronger. I still can't quite believe you can bury a tiny seed in soil and get something delicious you can eat a few months later. I still get a kick from the scent of tomato leaves and the sight of pearly new potatoes appearing out of dark soil. I still bore my friends with detailed accounts of my salad crop and how many zucchinis (courgettes) I picked for lunch. Only now I'm doing it on Instagram as well as on Twitter.

The world, though, has changed a lot since this book first came out (in 2009). Back then, growing vegetables was still largely the preserve of older people, mainly men. It had an old-fashioned vibe. Now hipsters from Brooklyn to Dalston of both sexes are well versed in the benefits of growing a little food, whether it's herbs, salad, or tomatoes. And every harvest and achievement can be posted on Instagram. Young mums juggle the school run with the garden plot. Community gardens in our cities include a vegetable garden almost as a matter of course. It's no longer odd to grow salad leaves outside the back door or on the balcony.

For me, back in my 20s, getting into growing food was I think some sort of reaction to the growing globalization of food production. In my small way, I felt that growing a few salad leaves was taking a bit of control back from what felt like a scarily monolithic system—the supermarket. We were concerned about fossil fuels and air miles with beans being flown across the world when they could just as easily be grown at home. It was also a reaction against the use of chemicals in intensive farming.

These concerns show no signs of going away, but I wonder if, for today's young people, there's an additional reason for the appeal of growing your own. Over the past 10 years or so the relentless dominion of screens in our lives pushes us ever more to enjoy the simple, slow pleasures of sowing, tending, pruning, and growing. And it's not just gardening. The whole area of domestic craft—home baking, sewing, and preserving—has had a shot in the arm over recent years thanks to the success of television shows such as *The Great British Bake Off*. It is no longer uncool to potter in your kitchen or garden, especially when the fruits of your labors can be #hashtagged into cyberspace. Spending time in the garden is not just weeding, it's mindful weeding. I will leave the irony of social media's influence in pushing the benefits of these slow pursuits to other minds to analyze!

Beets (beetroot) sown in pots with different spacings.

I suspect that, for new gardeners in the years to come, growing food will have another appeal as global awareness of the ills of plastic and how we dispose of it in the world becomes an increasingly hot topic. Any trip to the supermarket inevitably ends with half a bin full of plastic film, trays, and bags. Grow your own and you can avoid it.

Whatever it is that impels people to sow seed and grow food, we still need basic knowledge. And I hope that my 10 further years of growing food in various locations means this updated edition of my book is even more relevant to today's edible gardener. I have learned a lot along the way and I've inputted these changes accordingly. I've also included new discoveries to bring the growing tips right up to date.

This book was first published as *The Girl's Guide to Growing Your Own* because back in 2009, young women didn't really grow vegetables that much. The fact that this now seems strange is a wonderful thing. Since then I've written three more gardening books, but this one has a very special place in my heart because it's filled with the unbridled enthusiasm of the recent convert. With the addition of the benefit of retrospect and almost 10 years of sowing, growing, and harvesting, I hope it will be useful to anyone starting on this wonderful journey of growing food. Keep growing a little bit of what you eat, no matter how small your space. It doesn't have to take over your life, but I promise it will make your life feel a little better.

—Alex Mitchell

Introduction

I WASN'T ALWAYS THE SORT to wax lyrical over a lettuce leaf. A typical British child of the 1970s—the dawn of convenience food—I grew up eating boil-in-the-bag cod and baked beans. The nearest my mother got to growing her own peas was the frozen food aisles of our local supermarket. Now I eulogize cherry tomatoes, ponder over various types of kale, and am never happier than when wandering round my tiny garden picking sun-warmed strawberries. What on earth happened? Was it a reaction to living in a flat in north London in my mid-twenties, where the only wildlife was manky pigeons and the only greenery the plane trees in the street below? I started with window boxes of garish orange marigolds and red geraniums. Soon I graduated to arugula (rocket) and baby salad leaves. By the time I'd eaten my first homegrown tomato, I was hopelessly hooked.

As a journalist working on a tabloid newspaper alongside shouty, hard-drinking, hard-smoking hacks, I'd juggle my tomato growing bags with newspaper deadlines and keep my growing horticultural obsession quiet.

Ten or so years later and my passion for growing lovely things I can eat shows no sign of slowing down. But I'm no longer alone. Now I can hold my head high. We appear to be in the grip of a growing-your-own food revolution.

Why? We've now had a few years of enjoying exotic fruit in winter, strawberries all year round, and little green (French) beans lined up in perfect rows, trimmed for our convenience and flown in from Kenya. Yet something doesn't feel right. What about food miles, pesticides, packaging, organic food standards, the state of the farming industry? What's in those bagged salads? Most of all, what about taste? We've all eaten things that looked like strawberries, but tasted like, well, nothing at all. And when did peaches start resembling cotton wool?

Yet what's a modern eco-conscious urbanite to do? You might want to eat local, fresher, organically grown fruit and vegetables, but you don't want to move to the middle of nowhere, start wearing overalls, and become self-sufficient. You could get a community garden

Lettuce and Red Duke of York potatoes harvested in early summer.

My pots sown for spring.

plot, but even if you managed to get to the top of the waiting list before you're too old to lift a hand trowel, you might not want the hassle of travelling to a large plot some distance from your home that will need your attention come rain or shine the whole year round. You don't want to break your back digging and lugging heavy sacks or rigging up complicated wooden supports or nets. You want to carry on as you are, just with fewer trips to the supermarket and the pleasure of picking and eating your own fresh, organic produce with the minimum of effort.

This is the book I wish I'd had when I started growing my own. It's not for gardening nuts, it's for people who have busy lives but still like the idea of eating a fresh salad they've grown themselves, popping outside to get some herbs for a risotto, or eating deliciously ripe strawberries straight off the plant. How often do you see blue potatoes, stripy tomatoes, golden beets (beetroot), yellow snow peas (mangetout), or purple green (French) beans at your supermarket? Or, for that matter, trombone-shaped squashes, purple artichokes, and white eggplants (aubergines) flecked with the most delicate pink? You don't need a greenhouse or any fancy equipment to grow any of the plants in this book. With just a hand trowel, some seedlings, a few pots, and a bag of potting mix you can conjure a veritable harvest from a balcony or even a couple of windowsills. If you get yourself some nice gardening gloves—I defy anyone to say my pink-trimmed suede gauntlets are not objects of beauty—you won't even need to get dirt under your nails.

Getting Started

SOME CROPS ARE EASIER TO GROW than others. Sometimes I think you could throw arugula (rocket) seed into the wind and come back three weeks later and find a salad. Eggplants (aubergines), on the other hand, can refuse to produce unless they're showered with love and proverbial fan mail. To make it easier to choose what you might want to grow, I've only included crops that are easy to grow in small gardens and pots. I have, however, included a few demanding prima donnas. And when the result could be a warm, sun-ripened peach, a bowl of purple figs, or a sweet roasted red pepper, the rewards are worth it.

Symbols explained

 Tip from yours truly

 Project you can tackle in one weekend

 Recipe to test your gardening skills

 You couldn't kill it if you tried

 Reliable favorites—the horticultural equivalent of jeans and a T-shirt

Won't be taken for granted, but no prima donna either

 **High maintenance! (but super worth it)**

Right: Cilantro (coriander) flowering.

Top Crops for Different Plots

However large or small your growing space, there's a fruit or vegetable that you can grow in it. If you only have time for one crop, try these . . .

A balcony—tomatoes   (page 46)

Indoor windowsill—basil   (page 70)

Outdoor window box—peppers   (page 44)

A small back garden—kale   (page 68)

One big container—zucchini   (page 49)

Don't I Need to Buy Lots of Tools?

No. There will always be people who draw outlines of spades, hoes, and forks on their garden shed walls so they can hang their vast collection of tools in exactly the right place in order that they don't get mixed up or, God forbid, actually touch the floor. This is a conspiracy to make people think gardening is complicated. Here's the news, you don't need lots of tools and you really don't need a shed. Everything can be purchased online or bought on a quick trip to a garden center.

You will need . . .

For seed sowing, I use either small 3 in. (7.5 cm) plastic pots or seed starting trays—plastic grids of interconnected cells available from any garden center. These are great because, when it's time to transplant the seedlings, you just pop out the cell and plant the whole thing, so you don't have to worry about damaging the roots.

t How to transplant seedlings from seed starting trays

Getting plants out of pots without destroying them is a basic but much overlooked skill. It's no good grabbing the leaves and yanking—you're likely to leave the roots behind. But simply turning the pot upside down and shaking is likely to send the poor things flying to the ground in an ungainly tumble. Nowhere is this more sensitive than when dealing with seed starting or plug trays, those helpful little grids that are so good for starting off seeds, since when plants are still small they are even more vulnerable to user error. The best way to get your seedlings out intact is to give each cell a gentle squeeze to loosen the roots from the sides, then poke up through the drainage hole with a stick or the blunt end of a pencil. The whole plant, roots and all, should just pop out and you can then replant it into a bigger container, handling it by the rootball so you don't damage the plant itself.

Labels are good for reminding you what you've sown where (I'm constantly seeing lettuces poke up where peas should have been) and garden **twine** always comes in handy.

Otherwise, those gardening in containers can do everything they need with a **hand trowel**, some nice **pots**, and a **watering can** with a rose attachment (a perforated spout).

Those with a garden will need a **garden fork** and **spade** too.

Crops in Pots

Most fruit and vegetable crops can be grown in pots—in fact, some, like figs and blueberries, prefer it. A group of plants in containers can look as jungly as a garden border, and you can fit in masses on a small terrace, from herbs to fruit trees. In fact, pretty much any crop can be grown in a pot, if the pot is big enough. If you treat them as mini beds, cramming in different plants—salad leaves, zucchini (courgettes), and nasturtiums, say, or purple green (French) beans and California poppies at the base of a fig tree— pots can look surprisingly lush. Large terracotta pots, weathered with lichen, can be objects of beauty in themselves.

The best thing about growing in containers, though, is that you don't have to worry about your soil because you're not using it. Just buy some organic all-purpose potting mix to fill your pots with and you're good to go. And if you haven't time even to sow crops, you can buy them as seedlings and plant them straight out. It's pretty much instant gardening.

Any container can be used to grow plants as long as it has holes in the base for water to drain away. You could use an ice-cream tub if you wanted, though you may not thrill to the idea of a terrace full of things with Mint Choc Chip written on the side. If so, there are many options . . .

 ## "Crocks" in first

Every time you plant anything in a pot or window box, you'll hear about adding "crocks" to the bottom first. What on earth are they and do you really need to bother? Traditionally, they're bits of broken terracotta pot that stop the drainage holes from getting clogged up with soil and roots and waterlogging the plants. So, **they are kind of necessary**. But why would you want to smash a perfectly good pot? In ye olde times, large gardens might have had a constant supply of smashed terracotta (along with a constant supply of gardeners in waistcoats), but these days, with a small garden, you probably don't have any. I use a couple of handfuls of pea gravel (shingle) instead, along with any broken plastic pots. Stones are fine too. Or chuck in some broken-up pieces of Styrofoam (polystyrene). They're light, you can use them again and again, and, best of all, you'll get rid of some of that packaging that's been cluttering up your hall.

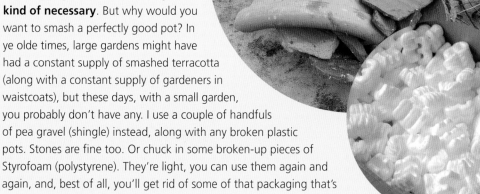

Terracotta. Old terracotta pots—with their faded charm and patina of lichen and calcification—are so much more appealing than the brand-new, orange, machine-made plastic things you find at big-box stores. For starters, they make it look like you've been gardening for ages so actually know what you're doing. To make them look older, mix some baking powder with a few drops of water to make a paste, and brush it onto the outside of the pots with a soft brush. Leave it to dry, then brush off any excess powder to leave a whiteish patina. To keep rain from washing away the powder, finish with hairspray or fixative. No one will ever know you didn't inherit them from dear old grandpapa's estate.

Glazed pots. These pots are for people who want to pretend they live in the Mediterranean, which is most of us. They usually come in deep vivid blues, turquoises, and greens.

Old wooden wine crates. These are perfect for salad crops—ask at your nearest wine store, they often have some they're throwing out. They're somehow the perfect size to grow a decent patch of greens or even tomatoes, and their imprinted logos give them a certain élan.

Fiber cement pots. Fiber cement (fibreclay) pots are also available, and are styled to look like lead. Light, large, and deep enough for fruit trees, they look just like those heavy lead planters you see in the gardens of stately homes with the bonus that you don't have to remortgage your house to buy them and they won't fall into your downstairs neighbor's breakfast.

t # 3 and 5 look better than 2 or 4

For some reason odd numbers of containers **always look better** than even ones—the same rule applies when planting seedlings out in the garden. Three or five plants make a nice cluster—a group of two or four looks contrived and unnatural.

t Sprinkle with pea gravel

Make crops in pots look the business by covering the top of the potting mix with a **layer of pebbles (shingle)**. It not only looks smart and reflects light, hiding all that dark earth, but also keeps moisture in the mix and thus reduces the amount of watering you need to do. A medium-sized bag of pea gravel is easy to find in garden centers and goes a very long way.

Or improvise. If you're feeling creative you can use anything—colanders, hats, teapots, even old boots—as growing containers. I've even seen strawberries growing happily in a leather handbag. Old farm (butler) sinks are popular but beware, they are incredibly heavy—and do add plenty of crocks and gravel (grit) at the bottom since the drain may not be enough for drainage. Some people seem to like the challenge of turning any old incongruous thing into a container. Tires, buckets, old bathtubs . . . I'm still scarred by memories of a friend who kept planting lobelia in a toilet. I sometimes think there's a fine line between creativity and a vacant lot that someone's dumped trash on.

Metal containers. Metal containers—for those aiming for a clean, modern look—work really well, whether galvanized tin, copper, zinc, aluminum, or brushed steel. Classic metal dustbins can look surprisingly smart, especially in a row of three. Even regular tin cans can be co-opted for growing herbs, salads, even hot peppers. Paint them with exterior masonry paint for a subtler effect or leave them to rust naturally. If you can find large, attractive, colorful cans—such as those used for olive oil or tomatoes in delis—they look great planted up.

Plastic. Brightly colored tubs with handles are a good size and easy to move around. If the bright colors offend you, choose black or disguise them with burlap (hessian sacking) or bamboo or reed screening cut to size (you can buy this from garden centers).

Hanging baskets: back in style

The only option for hanging baskets used to be the traditional rattan upturned dome, bursting out all over with clashing busy lizzies and geraniums like an over-exuberant hat. The recent houseplant revival has breathed new life into the humble hanging basket. Clay, plastic, even concrete planters suspended from the ceiling are adorning desirable interiors for the first time since the 1970s and, if you move them outside, they make ideal homes for tumbling tomatoes, strawberries, herbs, and baby salad leaves. Just make sure you don't hang them with string that will rot and break when it gets wet; metal chains and nylon or plastic string are best.

 ## Help hanging baskets hold water

The only problem with hanging baskets is that they dry out quickly in hot weather. Regular watering is therefore essential, but to make life a bit easier mix a handful of **water-retaining gel** into the potting mix when you plant them.

Grow bags always seem to thrive

They may be unfashionable, but I love grow bags. Long, plastic-wrapped sausages of potting mix, they're usually emblazoned with garish pictures of tomatoes and don't look very chic. However stylish your collection of weathered terracotta pots is, toss a growing bag in there and you'll really lower the tone. And yet they're so perfect for growing tomatoes in a small space that I use them every year. Nothing is easier than making three crosses in the plastic with a kitchen knife and then planting a tomato in each. They always seem to thrive, even if plants in the soil or other pots struggle.

But how to deal with that plastic? In an unusually industrious/creative moment, I had some shallow wooden boxes made, just the right size to fit the bags in. I then covered the bags with pea pebbles so you'd never know they were there. You can buy ready-made burlap (hessian) covers that will neatly slip over the grow bags, too, giving them a more natural look. Alternatively, display your garish, plastic grow bags with pride and tell anyone who criticizes them not to be such a terrible snob.

A window box for every window

Most people, even those who live in apartments, can have a garden. It's just that it might be three floors up and on your windowsill. Outdoor window ledges are great growing spaces. All you need is a window box.

I tend to avoid plastic window boxes because, however glorious the plants in them, all I can see is the ugly box. Terracotta and light metal ones always look good, wooden ones are great for a rustic look, and there are rattan ones for the folksy-devoted. But my current favorites are those made of fiber cement (fiberclay) styled to look like lead, large enough to hold plants like eggplants (aubergines) and peppers. Whatever you choose, get the biggest and deepest you can for your windowsill (weight restrictions permitting). Small, shallow boxes can dry out in a few hours on a hot summer's day—the larger the box, the less you'll be rushing back and forth with a watering can. Bespoke window boxes that fit your windowsill may be a worthwhile investment since they will maximize your growing space and look elegant. Check online for a supplier.

t Insulate window boxes

Metal window boxes are light and modern, but they tend to heat up in hot weather. This dries out the potting mix and can overheat the roots. Insulate the box against the sun by lining the inside (not bottom) of the box with any **sheets of Styrofoam (polystyrene)** you might have hanging around from packaging.

The heavier the window box, the less likely it is to blow off and knock someone out in the street below, but it's worth taking precautions however much you may dislike your downstairs neighbors. You can buy handy bracket and box kits that keep everything safely tethered or tie a sturdy chain around the box and attach it to the wall and sleep better on those windy nights.

Crops in Soil

Yes, I know, this is the boring part. Can't I just plant something in the earth as it is and hope for the best, you might be thinking? Well, you can, but you might not get very many tomatoes in return. I don't know, perhaps you have inherited your garden from a lovely old gent who has spent the past 40 years digging in manure, clearing weeds, and removing stones, leaving you with perfect soil that you can merely touch with a seed and cause a productive, edible jungle to grow. But it's highly unlikely. Chances are your garden, like most gardens, is a green rectangle of boggy lawn flanked by borders of limping shrubs, badly drained soil, a healthy army of weeds, and an abandoned bicycle (why do all gardens seem to contain an abandoned bicycle?).

So how do you transform it into a verdant paradise of tomatoes, sweet corn, salad, and beans?

 ## Raised bed kits

If you can't face preparing your soil for planting, there is a way out. Most garden equipment suppliers sell raised bed kits, basically shallow wooden or plastic squares that you fill with potting mix or topsoil. They work **like giant containers** and mean you don't have to be so vigilant about your garden soil since you're raising the level a good few inches. Just break up the earth at soil level before you put the raised bed on so you don't compromise drainage.

Raised bed kits are popular because they give the impression of instant gardening and look very neat and tidy. However, you will have to construct them so factor in some time and hassle. They also scream "Vegetable Plot!" so, if you're aiming for a more organic, mix-n-match look, combining flowers and vegetables in a cottage-garden style, they may not be for you.

Know thy soil

It's a gardener's maxim, often muttered by allotment veterans, master gardeners, and other know-it-alls that "look after your soil and the plants will look after themselves." They have a point. The first step to getting your soil ready to plant into is to find out what sort it is.

Pick up a small handful and try to form it into a ball shape between your palms. If it won't form a ball and feels gritty, it's sandy; if you can form it into a thick cylinder but not a thread, it's silty; if you can form it into a ring, then it's clay; if you can't form it into any shape at all, then it's a patio.

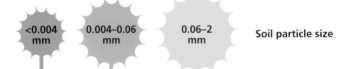

<0.004 mm **0.004–0.06 mm** **0.06–2 mm** **Soil particle size**

Sandy soil: Sandy soils have large particles and, like sand on a beach, allow water to drain through quickly. This means that they warm up quickly in the spring so you can start planting earlier than those with other soils. They are also easy to dig so your back will thank you. On the downside, nutrients get washed out of them so you need to add organic matter to slow this down as well as to prevent them from drying out in hot weather. Generally, though, this is one of the easiest soils to deal with, so well done you.

Silty soil: If your soil is silty, it will contain more nutrients than sandy soil yet still drain well. When dry, silty soils are smooth and look like dark sand. They are easy to work with when moist and hold moisture well but benefit from the addition of gravel or pebbles (grit) and organic matter.

Clay soil: Clay soil is often described as a "challenge," which is another way of saying, "poor you." However, if treated properly it can be the most fertile of all soils so persevere and you'll be rewarded. To understand why clay soil has this rather fearsome reputation, imagine digging a lump of sticky, wet clay with a trowel. It's the tiny particles that make up clay soil that make it so heavy since there is very little room for air pockets. When wet, it is very sticky; when dry it forms rock-hard clods. But, and here's the good news, clay soils naturally contain high levels of nutrients. So, if you can improve the drainage, you are onto a winner. Add lots of organic matter—manure or compost.

Chalky soil: Soil that is chalky is alkaline, light brown, and contains large quantities of stones. Basically, chalky soils are a bit rubbish, but not irredeemable. They dry out quickly and have a tendency to stop elements such as iron and manganese from getting to plants, which can cause poor growth and yellow leaves. Add lots of organic matter—this makes the soil slightly more acidic over time. Raised beds with imported topsoil may be worth it if troubles persist. Most fruit and vegetables prefer a neutral to slightly acidic soil with the exception of the cabbage family, which prefers it slightly alkaline.

Loamy soil: This is the crème de la crème of garden soils, the Olympic Gold of the earth world. A winning combination of sand, silt, and clay, loamy soil combines good drainage with an ability to hold on to nutrients well. If you have been working your garden soil for years, adding well-rotted manure and compost regularly, you may well have one of these soils. In which case, I envy you.

The great news about your soil is that all soils are redeemable with the addition of well-rotted farmyard manure or compost, both of which come under the general category of organic matter.

t Dig for victory—twice?

This is the sort of thing that some gardeners get very vexed about. They spend whole weekends digging trenches that reach almost as far as Australia (this is known as "double digging") and carefully sorting soil into topsoil and subsoil. Really, and I'm going to stick my neck out here, unless you're unfortunate enough to be gardening on a paddock compressed by a herd of cattle for the past ten years—double digging is unnecessary.

The only exception would be if you have a heavy clay layer under the topsoil that prevents water from draining away. This can cause waterlogging to plant roots so is best broken up with a garden fork. Adding some gravel or grit before replacing the topsoil will help drainage even further.

Much better to find a free 40 minutes and isolate a manageable area—perhaps nothing more than a square yard to start with. Dig down to the depth of a garden fork, removing any weeds and stones and breaking up lumps in the soil with the back of the fork. Then spread a layer of manure or compost about 4 in. (10 cm) thick on the top and fork it in. Ideally, you'd put the compost or manure on in the autumn and let it settle into the soil a bit before planting in spring, but any time of year is OK.

t The confusing business of soils

Beginners are often advised to add **compost** to improve the fertility of soil. What does this mean? Well, it means adding the rotted down contents of your compost pile—the heap of kitchen scraps, prunings, lawn cuttings, and old leaves in the corner of your garden. When rotted down, this mixture (sometimes called "garden compost" or "kitchen compost") is full of nutrients that will improve the soil fertility and improve drainage too. And if you don't yet have a compost pile? Then buy premade compost or composted manure from the garden center.

On the other hand if you are advised to fill a pot with **all-purpose potting mix** (known as **"multipurpose compost"** in England), do not head to your compost pile. Instead, buy a bag of potting or all-purpose mix from the garden center and use that. This is great for starting seeds and seedlings in but only has enough fertility in it to sustain a plant for around a month. It will do little to improve garden soil.

Soil could probably do with some clarification too. **Topsoil** is the uppermost layer of garden soil—around the top 12 in. (30 cm). This is where all the fertility and organic matter lies. Under this is the **subsoil**, low in nutrients and high in rocks and minerals. You don't want to grow vegetables in subsoil, so if you're preparing a new planting area make sure you leave the topsoil in position. If you're making raised beds, you can buy bags of topsoil from garden centers and this, mixed half and half with compost, would make the ideal starting mix.

Clear as mud?

Or compost?

t Is your soil sick?

Some urban areas, particularly those that were once industrial zones, have soil that is contaminated by lead or other pollutants. If you suspect this may be the case in your area, it would be safest to grow fruit and vegetables in raised beds or containers and save the soil for inedible ornamental plants only.

It's true: "grit" is useful

When I started this gardening lark there were times I thought I'd inadvertently wandered into a building supply store. What did coarse (sharp) sand and gravel (horticultural grit) have to do with pretty flowers and perfect raspberries? As for perlite, why would you put the contents of your beanbag in a vegetable bed?

Now that I'm older and a little bit wiser I know grit and coarse sand are added to heavy soils, such as clay, to let water drain through better and not waterlog the roots of plants. Coarse sand is used because it's quite coarse grained, so allows water to run through it better than finer varieties. Don't use beach or children's sandpit

sand because they contain salts that damage plants. Horticultural gravel or grit works in a similar way, opening up the soil and letting water drain through. If you have a heavy clay garden soil, it's worth a trip to a garden center or DIY superstore to get a bag or two of either.

Perlite, which looks like little Styrofoam (polystyrene) balls although it's actually made of volcanic rock, does the same thing but is used when planting in pots. It's worth adding a handful to the potting mix when you're planting things that hate being waterlogged, such as Mediterranean herbs, or those that will stay in the same pot for ages, like fruit trees.

Compost

"My whole life has been spent waiting for an epiphany, a manifestation of God's presence, the kind of transcendent, magical experience that lets you see our place in the big picture. And that is what I had with my first compost heap."

—Bette Midler

And who am I to argue with a legendary diva? Forget yoga and meditation, it seems that spiritual peace was always waiting for us in the shape of bits of old carrot. Who knew? Ever since I threw potato peelings, coffee grounds, dead plants, and slug-eaten lettuce leaves into a compost bin and got crumbly soil stuff out a year later, I've been a total composting maniac. Put the stuff on your garden and it makes everything grow bigger and better. It's organic, it's easy, and it's phenomenally satisfying in a circle-of-life kind of way.

Why would I want a smelly plastic thing cluttering up my garden when I've got a perfectly good rubbish collection service, you might think? My answer to this is that compost doesn't smell if you jab a garden fork into it now and then, and that my two white clapboard "beehive"-style compost bins (at right) are more stylish than my sofa—though that may say more about my sofa than my compost bins.

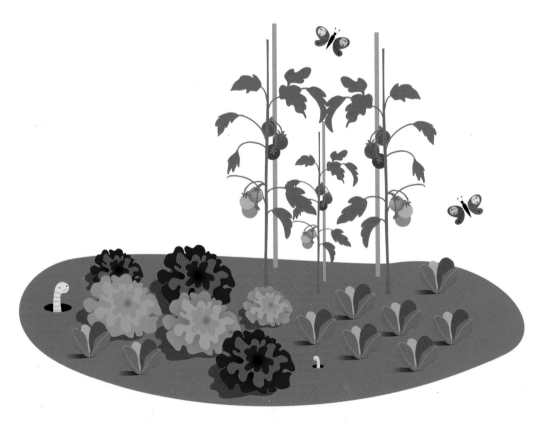

Some Composting Dos and Don'ts

DO compost uncooked vegetable peelings and scraps.

DO compost coffee grounds and tea bags (but take the tea leaves out first if you don't want to see the bag intact years later—they don't rot down).

DO compost lawn clippings, but try to add them in small quantities interspersed with cardboard torn up into hand-sized pieces to avoid sliminess.

DO compost leafy garden prunings.

DO compost cardboard and newspaper in small quantities torn up into pieces. You don't want to create a "mat" that will keep water from getting down to the contents below. Beware cardboard with a thin plastic film since this won't rot down and will come back to haunt you when you're digging.

DON'T compost cooked vegetable waste, meat, fish, or eggs.

DON'T compost flowering weeds and perennial weeds such as nettles unless you want to reintroduce them to the garden. Instead, either throw them away or soak them in a bucket of water for a week to kill them before adding them to the compost bin.

DON'T compost eggshells unless you are prepared to wash them first and risk attracting rats.

DON'T add avocado skins or pits (stones)—they take years to rot down.

DON'T compost large branches—they'll still be there when you're collecting Social Security.

Manure: what do you mean you don't know the whereabouts of your nearest defecating horse?

I did a garden course once in which the teacher mentioned well-rotted garden manure approximately every six minutes, like a sort of horticultural Tourette's. "Spread well-rotted garden manure over your soil in autumn," he would say, or "Be sure to incorporate plenty of well-rotted manure." (For some reason, manure is always "incorporated" in garden books, as though it's joining a company.) Even if I knew what this stuff was, I'd wonder, how can I locate it in an urban area when sightings of horses and cows are about as common as a street without a Starbucks? And how rotted is "well rotted?"

Basically, if it doesn't smell, it's well rotted. It's the manure of horses or cows mixed in with straw and left to rot down for at least a year, preferably two or three. When you add it to the soil, it helps water drain through and adds nutrients, particularly nitrogen, which promotes healthy green growth, as well as phosphorus and potassium, which stimulate root growth and fruit production. If you don't let it rot down first, it'll burn the plants and smell like a herd of cows has just used your garden as a lavatory, which in essence, they just have.

Before you set off in search of a police horse to walk behind carrying a large plastic container, you should know that you can buy well-rotted manure from garden centers in nice, clean plastic bags. There are also online companies that will deliver manure. But make sure it's a responsible company. A friend once opened the door to a smiling man offering well-rotted manure for sale. How nice, she thought, and got out her wallet. Ten minutes later a heap of steaming, stinking fresh manure was dumped all over her front garden. She spread it on her beds where it burned all the plants, turning the leaves yellow, so proving the maxim, never trust a man with dirty shoes.

Soil preparation in a nutshell

Figure out what sort of garden soil you have. **1**

2 Turn over about a garden fork's depth of soil, removing weeds and large stones and breaking up clods so you get a fine, crumbly texture.

Add a thick layer (at least 4 in. [10 cm]) of well-rotted manure or compost, loosely digging it into the earth. **3**

4 Have a nice cup of tea. Right, now that's all sorted, you're ready to actually plant something.

Spring

KICK OFF YOUR SHOES, get out your sunglasses, spring has sprung. Actually, on second thought, don't. The sun may be higher in the sky and new leaves unfurling, but spring can seem to take an agonizingly long time to get going. I used to get so excited at the first glimpse of a green leaf that I'd skip around the garden in a T-shirt, sowing beets (beetroot), carrots, and lettuce and pretending I wasn't getting hypothermia. Unsurprisingly, all the seeds rotted and died. It's better—and, let's face it, far less hassle—to sow a few things on a warm windowsill inside, nice and cozy, and plant them when you can go outside without your fingers going numb.

Beginning in early spring, beets, lettuces, and chard can be started in seed starting trays or little plastic pots inside. You can also lay out your potatoes to start "chitting." By mid-spring, it's time to plant potatoes, sow tomatoes, zucchini (courgettes), cucumbers, sweet corn, basil, green (French) beans, and peas inside and carrots, arugula (rocket), and radishes out. Don't feel you have to sow everything, turn your bathroom into a jungle, and crunch potting mix underfoot every time you get into the bath. A few pots are more than enough. There's only so much chard anyone can eat, after all. And, if sowing sounds too much like hard work, you can always buy ready-grown plants from garden centers or online in late spring.

By the end of the season, the garden is raring to go. You might be eating your first succulent baby fava (broad) beans in a warm salad with tiny new potatoes, roast mini beets, and feta. There's earthy kale for picking, refreshing radishes, fiery red radicchio, scallions (salad onions), cut-and-come-again salad, spicy arugula, chard, crunchy winter purslane, and mâche (corn salad). On warm days you can almost hear the plants growing.

If you do only three things this season:

PLANT

new (salad) potatoes

SOW

arugula (rocket)

SOW

lettuce

Arugula (Rocket)

Hard to believe, I know, but we did once eat salads without this peppery little leaf. These days, every supermarket salad bag contains it, a restaurant garnish isn't complete without it, and even pizzas come crowned with the stuff. We're addicted to arugula. Lucky it's so easy to grow then.

Sow it outside from mid-spring, straight into the pot or bit of ground you want to grow it in. It's super fast and needs no special attention. Arugula basically comes in two types: salad arugula, with its more rounded leaves and less peppery taste, which needs sowing every few weeks for a constant supply, and the hotter wild arugula with narrower, serrated leaves. This is a perennial so will last the whole growing season and might even survive until the following year. I grow both. Sow little and often, though. If your arugula starts tasting like someone's poured hot mustard powder into your mouth and your eyes start streaming, it's time to pull up the plants and start again.

Sowing arugula

When? Mid-spring to late summer

In Pots

medium-sized container with drainage holes • all-purpose potting mix • arugula seeds • 20 minutes

How? Sprinkle the seeds thinly over the surface, then cover with a thin layer of potting mix. Water. Place in a sunny or partially shaded spot.

In Soil

pencil or stick • arugula seeds • 10 minutes

How? With your pencil or stick, scratch a shallow groove in the soil. Sprinkle the arugula seed thinly along it, then cover with soil and water well.

What next? Keep moist and harvest leaves with scissors by cutting just above the smallest new leaf when the plants reach about 4 in. (10 cm) tall. The plants will then resprout two or three times before needing to be resown.

Where have I gone wrong? Flea beetle is the only real pest to watch out for.

New (Salad) Potatoes

Homegrown new or salad potatoes taste better than the ones from the store. They just do. They're fresher, earthier, and you can choose from some wonderful varieties. Above all, there's something very satisfying about upturning a bucket of potato plants on the patio and seeing the perfect spud treasure roll out to be made into a delicious potato salad there and then.

I only ever grow potatoes in containers since they grow so well this way. I also only grow new potatoes because the large ones for baking, mashing, and roasting are so cheap to buy and take so long to grow. Buy any first or second early potato variety from a garden center or online specialist.

My favorites are the classic salad spud 'Charlotte,' nutty 'Anya,' red 'Duke of York,' 'Ratte,' and knobbly 'Pink Fir Apple.' For a really early harvest, go for 'Swift' or 'Rocket.' For something different try 'Salad Blue' potatoes (see page 112) that make an unearthly but utterly delicious violet-colored mash. Eat your freshly dug spuds hot with butter, cold with mayonnaise, or in a warm salad with feta, chives, and baby beets. Glorious.

Planting potatoes

When? Start by laying them out for chitting on a light windowsill in early spring. By mid-spring they are ready for planting out.

In Pots

container with drainage holes • all-purpose potting mix • seed potatoes (preferably chitted, though this is not essential) • 20 minutes

"Chitting" potatoes

The world of potato growing seems to be riven with more jargon than that of any other vegetable. "Seed potatoes" are just potatoes you buy and plant to get more potatoes. If someone tells you they've been "chitting" in the greenhouse, don't call social services, they're merely placing their seed potatoes in a light place—windowsills are perfect—so that they can develop shoots so they get off to a head start. Potatoes are placed "rose end up"—so that the end with the beginnings of new shoots points up. People often use egg cartons for this, though don't feel you need to suddenly get through a dozen Columbian Blacktail eggs—any container that holds them upright will do. Leave them there for two or three weeks until the shoots or "chits" are an inch long. Then they're ready for planting.

Where? In any medium to large container (at least 10 in. [25 cm] diameter). You can use normal terracotta or plastic pots, or buy specially designed plastic potato barrels with lift-uppable sides. Growing new potatoes in pots is really popular, and there are loads of ingenious containers now available designed to look good and be easily movable. Some are bags made of thick-woven fabric, transformed into rustic beauty by woven willow surrounds. For sheer ease, you can't really beat "Spud Tubs," simple black plastic pots that are light to move around and have a certain minimalist appeal. They're perfect for those gardening on a balcony or terrace because you can roll them up and put them away when you're not using them. Pop three tubers in each.

How? Put a layer of crocks in the bottom of the container. Fill with 6 in. (15 cm) of all-purpose potting mix, and then place your potatoes on top of it with their chitted sprouts upwards. A 12 in. (30 cm) diameter pot would take two potatoes. Adjust the quantity of potatoes depending on how big your pot is. Cover with another 6 in. (15 cm) layer of potting mix. Water well. Place the container in a sheltered spot.

What next? When the shoots start to poke up through the mix, add enough mix to cover them. If frost is forecast, cover the shoots with newspaper or floating row cover (garden fabric). Keep piling on mix as the sprouts poke up and keep it all well watered. Eventually, the shoots will reach to the top of the pot and you'll have no more room to add mix. At this stage, start giving the pot a biweekly feed of tomato feed or liquid seaweed.

When will they be ready? It depends on the variety. Generally, first earlies take about ten weeks and second earlies about 13 weeks. Have a rummage around to check how they're getting along before impatiently upturning the whole pot. I can't count the number of times I've found garlic-clove-sized potatoes where proper-sized ones should be. It's worth pulling out just as many potatoes as you need for supper so the others can continue to grow.

Where have I gone wrong? The fungal disease called blight is the main potential foe of potatoes, though it's unlikely to be a problem with new potatoes. Other less serious problems may include common scab.

Lettuce

'Webb's Wonderful' lettuce, a very good, reliable variety.

Didn't lettuces used to be round, limp, and the consistency of chamois leather? They did in the 1970s, when a salad meant half a hard-boiled egg, some rock-hard tomatoes, and a few leaves of the green stuff, all smothered with salad dressing so vinegary it threatened your taste buds with eviction. How things change. These days, we're more likely to be eating Lollo Rossa than Iceberg, and the good old round lettuce has become almost fashionably retro. Frilly, crisp, red, green, blousy, pointy, frou-frou, or plain, it's a lettuce wonderland out there. Once you've eaten your own fresh lettuce, you'll never look at the chlorinated, supermarket pillow packs in the same way again.

Sow little and often and you can have fresh lettuce all year round. Whether it's a window box studded with five red and green oak-leafs,

a hanging basket out of reach of snails, or a few pots of mixed baby leaves on a balcony, lettuces are great for small spaces. Try them in a wooden wine crate (see page 16—salad leaves look rather stylish growing above a logo for Chateauneuf du Pape). Or intersperse different-colored lettuces in a checkerboard patch in a garden bed edged with spiky mizuna or arugula (rocket).

Either grow them to maturity and cut the whole thing, or sow them closer together and harvest with scissors above the smallest new leaf when they're still small. They'll resprout two or three times.

My favorite varieties are 'Webb's Wonderful,' 'Red Oak Leaf,' and 'Green Oak Leaf,' great either for baby leaves or mature heads, frilly 'Lollo Rossa' and 'Lollo Bianca,' and the sword-like 'Cocarde.' 'Little Gem' and 'Tom Thumb' are

Salad in a spin

Do yourself a favor, buy a salad spinner. When you've spent years buying ready-prepared salad in bags, it can be easy to forget that you actually might have to wash the stuff before eating. You don't need to eat waterlogged salad. A simple, plastic salad spinner gives you crisp, dry leaves in a few seconds.

particularly good for growing in pots and bring a nice, sweet crunchiness to sandwiches and salads. If you can't decide which varieties to buy, get a mixed packet and grow them as baby leaves.

For baby leaves

Lettuce grown in this way is great for all containers—from window boxes to hanging baskets. Simply snip after a few weeks and watch it regrow. You can buy some lovely mixed baby lettuce leaf selections, with all sorts of different shaped and colored leaves.

When? Mid-spring to early autumn.

In Pots

medium-sized container with drainage holes • all-purpose potting mix • lettuce seeds • 20 minutes

How? Sprinkle the seeds thinly over the surface, then cover with a thin layer of potting mix. Water. Place in a sunny or partially shaded spot.

In Soil

pencil or stick • lettuce seeds • 10 minutes

How? With your pencil or stick, scratch a shallow groove in the soil. Sprinkle the lettuce seed thinly along it, then cover with a thin layer of soil. Alternatively, sprinkle seed thinly wherever a gap appears in your bed and cover with a handful of all-purpose potting mix. Water well.

What next? Keep moist, and harvest leaves with scissors by cutting just above the smallest new leaf when the plants reach about 4 in. (10 cm) tall. The plants will then resprout two or three times before needing to be resown.

For mature lettuces

Baby leaves are all very well, but you sometimes want some crunch in a salad, something with a heart. Grow lettuces to maturity, and you can either harvest the whole thing at once or cut the outer leaves for sandwiches and salads as and when you want them. If you want a constant supply throughout the summer, resow when your seedlings have four leaves.

In Seed Starting Trays

seed starting tray • all-purpose potting mix • lettuce seeds • 30 minutes

Where? In a seed starting tray (a grid of plastic cells available from garden centers). For spring sowings, pop the seed starting tray on a sunny windowsill inside; in early summer move it outside.

How? Almost fill the tray cells with potting mix and tap the tray on the table gently to settle the mix. Place in a sink of water until the surface is moist or water from above with a watering can, then leave for a few minutes to drain. Sow two lettuce seeds on the surface of each cell, then barely cover with more potting mix.

What next? When the seedlings are big enough to handle, remove the weaker one. Then, when your seedlings have five leaves, transplant them either to larger containers or garden soil, at a spacing of about 12 in. (30 cm). Harvest them before they bolt (get leggy and sprout upwards as if trying to take off), when the leaves will start tasting bitter.

Where have I gone wrong? Watch out for slugs and snails, downy mildew, and botrytis.

t How to harvest lettuce

Cut-and-come-again lettuce

Sow about 1 in. (3 cm) apart and when the plant is about 4 in. (10 cm) high, harvest the top, cutting just above the smallest new pair of leaves. The plant will then resprout from here and can be harvested once or even twice more. This will give you small, fresh leaves ideal for adding to salads, garnishes, and sandwiches. Best for small spaces.

Harvesting "around" the lettuce

Sow lettuce 8 in. (20 cm) apart and let them grow to maturity. Once they have bulked up nicely, you can start taking the outside leaves, tearing or cutting them gently away at the base and leaving the rest of the lettuce intact. You can continue to take two or three leaves this way every few days while the lettuce continues to grow. Once the middle of the lettuce starts to shoot upwards, though, stop harvesting, since it is now bolting and the leaves will start to taste bitter.

Harvesting the whole lettuce

Sow lettuce 8 in. (20 cm) apart and let them grow to maturity. Then cut the whole lettuce off at ground level with pruners (secateurs) or a sharp kitchen knife, or simply pull up the whole plant. This is my favorite way to harvest lettuces because you get a good range of leaves, from the outer, green ones to the crunchy, sweeter inner leaves that make the tastiest salad. Best if you have a bit more space.

have an established compost bin, just chuck a few garden forkfuls of well-rotted stuff around the base of the plants or tree, called "side-dressing." If your compost has yet to rot down, it's worth buying a few bags of well-rotted manure or mushroom compost from a garden center instead.

Inside: a sweet way to banish a gloomy early spring day

In early spring, there are days the outside world looks so gray and barren all you want to do is get on a plane and escape the gloom. It's at times like this that I indulge in a little bit of comfort sweet pea sowing, aided and abetted by a large glass of wine and the cheesiest radio station I know, turned up high.

You will need

- 3 in. (7.5 cm) pots
- all-purpose potting mix
- 1 packet of sweet pea seeds
- 20 minutes

Outside: Top up those ever-growing fruits

Many established crops such as strawberries, blueberries, raspberries, blackberries, figs, and peaches could do with a mulch of garden compost or well-rotted manure in early spring. It helps keep moisture around the roots and provides nutrients to encourage healthy new fruits to grow. If you

My peas starting to climb.

Fill the pots almost to the top with potting mix and then push three seeds into each pot to the depth of your middle finger joint. Cover with potting mix, water, and place on a sunny windowsill, while singing along to a pop song you would never admit to liking in public. Keep well watered to avoid powdery mildew. When the seedlings have emerged and have two sets of leaves, pinch out the growing points. This may seem ruthless, but it will make the plant much sturdier so it's well worth doing. Leave the seedlings to grow until mid- to late spring, and then plant them at the foot of tripods, trellises, or hazel twigs, up which they'll scramble like fleet-footed little mountaineers.

Beets (Beetroot)

Banish all thoughts of the brutal vinegar-soaked purple wedges of your childhood. Homegrown beets, harvested small, roasted, and added whole to a warm late-spring salad, are a different thing altogether—famously sweet and aromatic. Or leave them until summer and slice them to show off their vivid hearts. Sow 'Bolthardy' or 'Darko' for deep red roots with the bonus of striking red leaves or 'Burpee's Golden' for golden yellow. My favorite, though, is 'Chioggia,' which, when sliced, reveals perfect concentric rings of red and white that make salads look a bit special. If you slice them thinly enough, they are great raw. You can also eat the young leaves and stems in salads. I like growing them in medium-sized pots, or they look just as good in rows or clumps in the border.

Sowing beets

When? Early spring in seed starting trays inside, mid-spring to midsummer outside.

In Seed Starting Trays

seed starting tray • all-purpose potting mix • beet seeds • 20 minutes

How? Almost fill the tray cells with potting mix. Water and leave to drain. Sow four seeds per cell, covering with ½ in. (1 cm) of potting mix. Place on a sunny windowsill inside.
What next? Keep moist. When the seedlings are 2 in. (5 cm) high, plant in soil or pots outside, allowing 4 in. (10 cm) between each.

In Pots

medium-sized container with drainage holes • all-purpose potting mix • beet seeds • 20 minutes

How? Sprinkle your seeds thinly over the surface, then cover with a thin layer of potting mix. Water. Place in a sunny or partially shaded spot.

In Soil

pencil or stick • beet seeds • 10 minutes

How? With your pencil or stick, scratch a shallow groove in the soil. Sow seeds about 2 in. (5 cm) apart. Cover with soil and water well.

What next? Pull up the beets when they're golf-ball sized.
Where have I gone wrong? Watch for slugs and snails and leaf miner. Plants can "bolt" (run to seed before growing a root) if they get too dry so keep them well watered.

Chard

Every community gardener grows it, CSAs (veg box schemes) are rarely without it, and at farmers' markets you can't move for the stuff. Chard is certainly popular to grow, but what do you do with it and does anyone actually want to eat it? "Looks pretty but I don't think anyone actually likes it," said a friend when I mentioned it the other day.

It's true that chard isn't everyone's favorite. But if you like spinach, you'll probably like it. Why not just grow spinach then, you might wonder. Well, because spinach is hard to grow—it runs to seed at the slightest change in temperature and needs constant moisture around its roots. The exception, and a crop well worth growing, is its relative, perpetual spinach, which despite its name is not a spinach at all. This useful crop will keep producing lush green leaves and stems for months and is just as happy in a window box as it is in the ground.

Chard thrives on neglect, grows through a drought, and would probably survive a brutal attack with a garden hoe. Even those who don't admire chard's culinary virtues have to admit that it's a beautiful-looking plant, with lush, deep green leaves and Day-Glo midribs of pink, yellow, or orange worthy of fluorescent highlighter pens. One plant will also last for months. Cut the outer leaves as and when you want them and the plant will, triffid-like, keep on producing more. Cut the leaves when small for salads, or steam big leaves and dot with melted butter and freshly ground black pepper.

For color, go for 'Bright Lights' or Rainbow chard. Gourmets prefer the classic Swiss chard with thick, white stems. Sown again in late summer or early autumn, a few plants dotted throughout the border are a very welcome sight in the lean times of winter.

Sowing chard

When? Early spring in seed starting trays inside, mid-spring to late summer outside

In Seed Starting Trays

seed starting tray • all-purpose potting mix • chard seeds • 20 minutes

How? Almost fill the tray cells with potting mix. Water and leave to drain. Sow one seed per cell, covering with ½ in. (1 cm) of potting mix. Place on a sunny windowsill inside.
What next? Keep moist. When the seedlings are 2 in. (5 cm) high, plant in garden soil or pots outside, allowing at least 8 in. (20 cm) between them.

In Pots

medium to large container with drainage holes • all-purpose potting mix • chard seeds • 20 minutes

How? Sow seeds ½ in. (1 cm) deep about 4 in. (10 cm) apart. Cover with potting mix, water well, and place in a sunny, sheltered spot. When the seedlings are big enough to handle, thin them to 8 in. (20 cm) apart. Allow three plants to a 12 in. (30 cm) diameter pot.

In Soil

pencil or stick • chard seeds • 10 minutes

How? Choose a sunny or partially shaded spot with well-cultivated soil. Make ½ in. (1 cm) deep holes with your pencil or stick about 12 in. (30 cm) apart. Pop one seed in each hole, then cover with soil and water well.

What next? Keep the plants well watered. Pick off the outside leaves as and when you want them for cooking, or pick them when they're small and eat raw in salads.

Where have I gone wrong? Watch young plants for slugs and snails and leaf miner.

Peppers

A pepper plant laden with green, orange, and red peppers is wonderfully exotic and cheerful. So seductive are these plants that I grow hot peppers every year even though neither I nor anyone in my household has ever eaten anything spicier than a chicken korma.

If you enjoy burning your taste buds to oblivion, there's a dizzying range of hot pepper seeds out there to buy, from mild 'Hungarian Hot Wax,' through Mexican 'Jalapeño' right up to the tiny but mighty hot Thai bird's eye chili peppers. I've had success with 'Etna,' though do a browse online since new varieties are being introduced all the time. Particularly good for pots and window boxes are 'Apache' and 'Thai Hot.'

In a northern climate, they're best grown in containers so they can be moved inside in late summer for the peppers to fully ripen. They look great in brightly colored pots or even metal pails and also do well in large window boxes. Start them off in early-mid spring and you'll be eating them by early autumn. If you can't handle all those fresh hot peppers at once, dry them in a cool oven and then keep in an airtight jar to crumble into curries, stir-fries, and sauces whenever you feel the need. Just be sure to wash your hands before rubbing your eyes!

As for sweet peppers, plant them in a pot and choose the sunniest, most sheltered site possible for these hot-blooded creatures. They particularly like growing bags (three to a bag), where the fertilized potting mix provides them with lots of potash to encourage the growing fruits. But they'll also be happy in a large pot or window box where their large fruits look impressively exotic. All sweet peppers start green and then ripen through yellow and orange to red, getting sweeter the redder they are. The compact 'Redskin' and 'Antohi Romanian' are great for growing in pots. Or try 'Marconi Rosso' in growing bags for a tapered, long Italian variety.

Sowing peppers

When? Early-mid spring
Where? Inside on a sunny windowsill

In Pots

3 in. (7.5 cm) pots • all-purpose potting mix • hot or sweet pepper seeds • 30 minutes

How? Three-quarters fill your pots with potting mix. Place two seeds on the surface of the potting mix in each pot. Cover with a thin layer of potting mix and water.
What next? When the seedlings are 1 in. (3 cm) tall, remove the weaker one.

Keep the seedlings in as sunny a spot as possible, turning the pots regularly to keep them from growing crooked towards the light. Keep the potting mix moist but not waterlogged. For planting out instructions, see Planting out seedlings, page 88.
Where have I gone wrong? Watch young plants for aphids and slugs and snails, which can make holes in the peppers.

Tomatoes Part 1

If I could only grow one thing in my garden, it would be tomatoes. It's a no-brainer. I know people always say that homegrown vegetables taste better, but in the case of tomatoes, they really do. However good the store-bought vine tomatoes now are—and unmistakable strides have been made since those scarlet ping-pong balls of my childhood—none can compare with a homegrown tomato, warmed by the sun. They smell wonderful, they look great, and they taste out of this world.

I stick to cherry varieties since I find these easiest to grow outside. The perennial old reliables 'Gardener's Delight' and 'Sungold' have never let me down. The golden-colored Sungolds, particularly, rarely make it into the house. A salad of Sungolds mixed up with red cherry tomatoes looks and tastes fantastic. But you could also try baby plum tomatoes such as 'Santa,' the red-and-yellow striped 'Tigerella' or impress discerning friends with 'Black Krim,' a Russian beefsteak tomato with a purple blush.

Upright or vining (cordon) types grow straight upwards and look great tied to trellises or fences, their fruits arching out on trusses among the vivid green leaves. Bush or trailing types sprawl over the sides of pots or window boxes or trail down gorgeously from hanging baskets.

You can buy tomato plants at garden centers from late spring to midsummer. However, if you want to grow unusual varieties (such as 'Sungold' or 'Tigerella') or simply like the idea of growing your own from scratch, then sow them on a sunny windowsill in mid-spring.

Sowing tomatoes

When? Mid-spring
Where? Inside on a sunny windowsill

In Pots

several small pots (3 in. [7.5 cm] ones are ideal)
• all-purpose potting mix • tomato seeds •
20 minutes

How? Three-quarters fill your pots with potting mix and stand them in an inch or so of water (the kitchen sink is ideal) until the surface of the mix is damp. Remove from the water to drain for a few minutes. Place two seeds on the surface of the mix in each pot. Cover with a thin layer of mix.
What next? Over the next few days, don't let the potting mix dry out. After about a week, your tomato seedlings will emerge. Continue to keep the mix moist but not wet and turn the tray regularly so that the seedlings don't grow crooked towards the light. When the seedlings are about 1 in. (3 cm) high, remove the weaker seedling in each pot. If your tomato seedlings start looking stretched and weedy, don't worry. Simply replant them in another pot so that the seed leaves (the bottom pair) are resting on the mix. New roots will soon grow from the buried stem. For planting out instructions, see Tomatoes Part 2, page 77.

Clockwise from top: 'Rosella,' 'Sungold,' 'Gardener's Delight.'

Know your tomatoes

Bush
Aka "determinate" because they reach a certain height and then stop. No need to pinch out or tie to supports, though they may benefit from being propped up with sticks if they get top heavy.

Vining or trellising (cordon)
Aka "indeterminate" or climbing because they will keep on going if you let them. Grow in grow bags, containers, or the ground and tie the central stem to a bamboo cane or to a string tied to an overhead support. Once the plant has formed five trusses of fruit, pinch out the top of the plant so it puts its energy into ripening the fruit it has already made. Also pinch out side shoots as they form.

Tumbling
Best for hanging baskets where they will trail over the edges. A good variety is 'Tumbling Tom.'

Cherry
Small, the size of a cherry, tomatoes. Because of their size they are the most reliable to ripen outside and are often the sweetest of the tomatoes.

Plum
These tomatoes are often used in sauces because they have a higher proportion of flesh to seed and juice.

Beefsteak
Large tomatoes great for slicing in sandwiches or salads. Northern climates may struggle to ripen these large tomatoes unless they are grown in greenhouses.

Cucumbers

I thought I didn't like cucumbers much. They were watery, tasteless things wrapped in plastic. But then I grew a few outdoor cucumber plants and I'm now a bona fide cucumber bore. The plants are pretty, climbing up a tripod or trellis with yellow flowers and lush green leaves, but it's the cucumbers themselves that are the real surprise. They have none of the wateriness of the store-bought kind, and a far more satisfying, sweet flavor. Grow 'Burpless Tasty Green' or a miniature variety such as 'La Diva' up a trellis. Or try the compact, non-climbing 'Bush Champion' if you're growing in a container. They make the perfect cucumber sandwich or grate them for amazing tzatziki.

Sowing cucumbers
When? Mid-spring
Where? Inside on a sunny windowsill

In Pots

3 in. (7.5 cm) pots • all-purpose potting mix • cucumber seeds • 20 minutes

How? Fill your pots almost to the top with potting mix. Push two seeds, on their sides, 1 in. (3 cm) deep into each pot. Cover with potting mix and water.
What next? When the seedlings are 1 in. (3 cm) tall, remove the weaker one. Keep moist. For planting out instructions, see Planting out seedlings, page 87.

Zucchini (Courgettes)

Whole books are published on the subject of how to cope with the enormous surplus of zucchini that you will apparently produce from your homegrown plants. This can give you the impression that you've failed if your plant isn't producing enough to run a small farm shop on a daily basis. Certainly, my plants have never read these books because they only seem to produce enough for a couple of people. Which is best, really, because I'm not too keen on zucchini chutney.

I love the huge, lush, sandpapery leaves, the cheerful, blousy, yellow flowers—apparently delicious deep-fried and stuffed with ricotta if you're feeling confident with a deep-fat fryer—and the way the little fruits seem to appear overnight. In a soup with chicken stock, rice, and lemon zest or just sliced lengthwise and griddled with olive oil and a spritz of lemon juice, they are mighty fine.

Zucchini comes in two types: bushes and climbers. With their prolific flowers and eye-catching fruits, climbing varieties look verdant clambering over a trellis, arch, or pergola, or up a trellis. Try 'Black Forest' or the wonderful 'Tromboncino' with its extraordinary long snake-like fruits that, if left to mature like a squash, are delicious. Bush types work better in pots or sprawling over a garden bed. 'Defender' is a good reliable variety, as is 'El Greco' and 'Tuscany,' which is compact so particularly good for containers. But for something unusual try the round 'Eight Ball,' yellow 'Gold Rush,' or 'Soleil,' or a stripy zucchini such as 'Romanesco.'

Sowing zucchini

When? Mid-spring
Where? Inside on a sunny windowsill

In Pots

3 in. (7.5 cm) pots • all-purpose potting mix • zucchini seeds • 20 minutes

How? Fill your pots almost to the top with potting mix. Push one seed, on its side, 1 in. (3 cm) deep into each pot and cover with potting mix. Water well.

What next? Keep moist. When roots start to show through the bottom of the pot, transplant each zucchini plant into a larger pot. For planting out instructions, see Planting out seedlings, page 87.

Squashes and Pumpkins

Dotted with orangey-yellow fruit and trailing around a terrace, a pumpkin or squash vine is the plant world's version of fairy lights. These are large, handsome plants, not to be confined. They like to sprawl, climb, trail, and colonize. And, in return, they'll give you fiery-skinned squashes with nutty flesh just crying out to be roasted and swathed in melted butter, turned into mouthwatering soups, or turned into fierce jack-o'-lanterns for Halloween.

The squashes split into two types. Summer squashes you eat straight off the plant in summer—such as the custard-yellow 'Sunburst.' Winter squashes, such as butternut, have a hard skin and keep for a few months. These include the peculiar but delicious spaghetti squash. Microwave it whole (pierce it first if you don't want it to explode!) then eat its pasta-like strands with butter. Utterly delicious. Or there's red, pear-shaped 'Uchiki Kuri' and 'Blue Hubbard' with its bright blue skin and yellow flesh, said by many to be the best-tasting of all.

If you're a pumpkin fan, choose 'Jack O'Lantern' for your perfect Halloween specimen, 'Rouge Vif d'Etamps' for a giant fit for Cinderella's carriage and, for pots, the mini 'Baby Bear'—the seeds of which can also be toasted as a nice snack.

Sowing squashes and pumpkins

When? Mid-spring
Where? Inside on a sunny windowsill

In Pots

3 in. (7.5 cm) pots • all-purpose potting mix • squash or pumpkin seeds • 20 minutes

How? Fill your pots almost to the top with potting mix. Push two seeds, on their sides, 1 in. (3 cm) deep into each pot. Cover with potting mix and water.

What next? When the seedlings are 1 in. (3 cm) tall, remove the weaker one. Keep moist. When roots start to show through the bottom of the pot, transplant each squash or pumpkin plant into a larger pot. For planting out instructions, see Planting out seedlings, page 88.

Eggplants (Aubergines)

Let's not kid ourselves: if you live in a northern climate you're never going to be able to grow eggplants as easily as you could in the Mediterranean or Middle East. But that just means making sure you choose a variety that's been bred for your climate and that produces small fruits, as opposed to enormous things that won't ripen properly. These small eggplants are wonderfully tender in stews like ratatouille or as shish kebabs on a barbie with halloumi cheese and zucchini. Plant a "baby" variety such as 'Ophelia' or 'Orlando' in a container and put it in the sunniest spot you can find. Buy plants in early summer if you'd rather not grow them from seed.

Sowing eggplants

When? Early to mid-spring
Where? Inside on a sunny windowsill

In Pots

3 in. (7.5 cm) pots • all-purpose potting mix • eggplant seeds • 30 minutes

How? Three-quarters fill your pots with potting mix. Place two seeds on the surface of the potting mix in each pot. Cover with a thin layer of potting mix and water.

What next? When the seedlings are 1 in. (3 cm) tall, remove the weaker one. Keep the seedlings in as sunny a spot as possible, turning the pots regularly to stop them from growing crooked towards the light. Keep the potting mix moist but not waterlogged. For planting out instructions, see Planting out seedlings, page 88.

Where have I gone wrong? Watch for aphids.

Celebrate Spring with a Salad Box

All it takes to grow a perpetually delicious salad bar is an outside windowsill. Take one large window box with drainage holes, add a layer of crocks to the bottom of the box, and fill almost to the top with all-purpose potting mix and voila, you're ready to go. Now take a look at that windowsill and see how much sun it's getting . . .

SUNNY SILL:
the impatient salad box

Here's one for the itchy-fingered. Sow these fast-growing crops in a window box from mid-spring on and you'll have the earliest harvest possible. Pop them on a sunny, sheltered window ledge outside for a peppy, crunchy salad for the new season.

You will need
- 1 packet of radish seed such as 'French Breakfast'
- 1 packet of arugula (rocket) seed
- 1 packet of mixed lettuce seed
- 30 minutes

Roughly dividing the box into three portions, thinly sprinkle the radish, arugula and lettuce seed onto the mix. Cover with a thin layer of mix, water well and place on a sunny, sheltered windowsill. Keep moist.

When the seedlings emerge, thin the radishes to 1 in. (3 cm) apart. Harvest by cutting the arugula and lettuce leaves above the smallest new leaf, and the radishes by pulling them up when they are big enough to eat.

SHADY SILL:
the earthy salad box

Even a shady sill can be used to grow salad. In fact, some things positively prefer to be out of the sun. Blood-veined sorrel has beautiful dark green leaves etched with purple veins and adds a deliciously citrus tang to salads. The spiky chives behind with their purple pom-pom flowers and interspersing of red and green lettuce in front complete the picture.

You will need
- 1 blood-veined sorrel plant (*Rumex sanguineum*)—if you can't find this, try the low-growing Buckler leaf or French sorrel rather than the more leggy Broad-leaved sorrel
- 2 chive plants
- 3 green lettuce seedlings, such as 'Green Salad Bowl' or 'Lollo Biondi'
- 2 red lettuce seedlings, such as 'Red Salad Bowl' or 'Lollo Rossa'
- 45 minutes

Plant the sorrel in the center at the back and the chives on either side. Then plant the lettuces, alternating in color, along the front of the box. Firm around the plants with more potting mix and then water well. Keep moist.

Either snip off individual leaves from the lettuces as and when you want them or wait until they are mature and harvest them whole.

Carrots

Juice them, dip them in hummus and tzatziki, make cakes out of them, or just pull them up and eat them after washing the soil off under the garden faucet. Carrots are to be filed in that category of vegetables you thought you didn't rate that much until you grew them yourself. It's something to do with the sugar, no doubt, that turns to starch soon after picking. A freshly picked one really does have the edge on a store-bought variety, with a sweetness that is addictive, particularly if you grow the tender, early varieties recommended below.

Grow them in the garden soil, in window boxes, or in pots. They're slow growing, but harvest them small and you'll really get the benefit of their crisp sweetness. I sow a couple of big pots of them in early spring for sweet baby roots that we eat raw or lightly steamed.

Try 'Amsterdam Forcing' or 'Early Nantes' for sweet, crunchy roots ready in 12 weeks. 'Atomic Red' and 'Yellowstone' will give you colorful alternatives, while for pots or window boxes the small round 'Paris Market' is a good choice. 'Chantenay' has highly flavored stubby roots, great for slow cooking in stews.

Sowing carrots

When? Mid-spring to midsummer

In Pots

medium to large container with drainage holes • all-purpose potting mix • carrot seeds • 20 minutes

How? Add a layer of crocks to the bottom of the container and then fill it almost to the top with potting mix. Sprinkle the carrot seeds thinly over the surface and barely cover with potting mix. Water well and place in a sunny, sheltered position.

In Soil

pencil or stick • carrot seeds • 10 minutes

How? Choose a sunny or partially shaded spot in well-cultivated soil that hasn't had manure or compost recently added (carrots don't like it). With your pencil or stick, scratch a shallow groove in the soil. Sprinkle the carrot seed thinly along it, then cover with soil and water well.

What next? When the seedlings are big enough to handle, thin them to about 2 in. (5 cm) apart. Investigate how big the roots have become, and pull them up when you like the look of them.

Where have I gone wrong? Carrot fly is the main pest, but slugs and snails can also be a menace to germinating seedlings.

Sweet Corn

Freshly picked, homegrown sweet corn is the supermodel of the edible gardening world. The ultimate in growing-your-own showing off is ripping cobs off the plant and throwing them straight on the barbie.

When picked and eaten quickly before the sugars have had time to turn to starch, sweet corn is inestimably delicious. Unfortunately, there is a slight catch. Like a reality TV star, sweet corn is high-maintenance, demanding, and prone to throwing hissy fits. It needs a sunny site in deep soil (so not one for containers) in order to develop decent-sized, ripe corncobs. It needs to be planted close together in a grid because it's wind pollinated and needs the flowers at the tops of the plants to shed their pollen onto the tassels below. Allow for at least 12 plants for a decent chance. Most of all, though, it needs a long, hot summer.

But if you pull it off, the rewards are enormous. Not only do you get a taste to die for, but the plants bring a certain exotic flavor to the garden, with their lofty stems, dangly tassels on top, and bulging cobs with their silks bursting out from the ends. Don't bother with those varieties called mini corn or baby corn, though. Even if they grow successfully, you'll only have enough for a small stir-fry.

Sowing sweet corn
When? From mid-spring on
Where? Inside on a sunny windowsill

In Pots

3 in. (7.5 cm) pots • all-purpose potting mix • sweet corn seeds • 20 minutes

How? Fill your pots almost to the top with potting mix and then push one sweet corn seed into each pot to a depth of about ½ in. (1 cm). Water.
What next? Keep the seedlings moist and plant them outside in soil in early summer. For planting out instructions, see Planting out seedlings, page 89.

Radishes

They're the sprinters of the vegetable world yet radishes are easy to dismiss. I always used to put them in the category of things schoolchildren might grow in "Veg Corner"—"Good boy, Raffie, look what you grew!"—but actually, a few crisp radishes sliced into a salad or sandwich or just eaten whole can be delicious. Dip them in unsalted butter and then into flakes of sea salt for a simple treat or use them in stir-fries. And remember, you can eat the leaves, too—they make a great soup. Best thing of all, though, is that they're one of the earliest crops you can harvest. 'French Breakfast' is long enough for slicing, with a pretty white tip. Real show-offs would go for a packet of multicolored 'Bright Lights' and pep up their salads with red, white, purple, and even yellow ones.

Sowing radishes

When? From mid-spring on

In Pots

container with drainage holes • all-purpose potting mix • radish seeds • 20 minutes

How? Add a layer of crocks to the bottom of the container and then fill it almost to the top with potting mix. Sprinkle the seeds on the top, about 1 in. (3 cm) apart, then cover with ½ in. (1 cm) of mix. Water. Place in a sunny or partially shaded spot.

In Soil

pencil or stick • radish seeds • 10 minutes

How? Choose a sunny or partially shaded spot with well-cultivated soil. With your pencil or stick, scratch a shallow groove in the soil. Sprinkle the radish seed along it about 1 in. (3 cm) apart, then cover with soil and water well.

What next? Keep moist. After about three weeks, investigate how big the radish bulbs have become and pull them up when you like the look of them.

Keep sowing every few weeks for a constant supply of radishes throughout the summer.

Garden Villains

Villain No. 1: slugs and snails

You may think you like animals. You may even cry at ads for animal cruelty on cable channels on TV. Once you've sown your first seed, though, there's one group of animals you'd gladly see squirming in salt: slugs and snails.

These voracious destroyers of plant life will turn the most mild-mannered, live-and-let-live type to a blank-eyed assassin. They crawl out from their secret hiding places at night and lay waste to seedlings in a few hours. They bite cleanly through the stems of runner bean plants, make lettuces disappear overnight, and cover your precious seedlings in slime, eating their tips so they rot and die. I don't consider myself particularly evil, but I've been known to cut slugs in half with pruners and enjoy it.

Sentimentalists think they can just throw them over the garden fence. It doesn't work. I've heard of people dabbing whiteout onto snails' shells and throwing them as far away as they can, only to see those same whited-out snails reappearing in their garden the next evening. These creatures aren't stupid.

The best way to avoid slug and snail damage is to grow your crops in pots or high out of reach in hanging baskets or window boxes. They may be clever, but they haven't yet learned to fly. If you're growing crops in the soil, you could try any one of the countless methods frequently attempted by the slug-desperate and snail-deranged.

What do you do about it?

- **Melon or grapefruit skins.** Pop these out at night and in the morning you'll find a nice little colony of slugs and snails enjoying a light breakfast. You can then dispose of them in the trash. This seems OK, but there's only so much grapefruit you can eat.
- **Beer traps.** Plastic traps you fill with beer. Come morning you find lots of drunk and dead slugs and snails that you dump into the trash. Not bad, but you won't catch them all this way.
- **Ground eggshells.** Utterly useless in my opinion.
- **Coffee grounds.** Ditto.
- **Nematodes.** These are microscopic natural predators that kill slugs for you. The slug nematode (*Phasmarhabditis hermaphrodita*) is a teeny eelworm that releases bacteria into slugs, which kills them. Nematode products come as beige powders that you mix up in a watering can and sprinkle onto the soil. There's something undeniably satisfying about unleashing a righteous army of soldiers, even if they are invisible to the naked eye.
- **Nightly trips outside** with a flashlight and a large bowl of hot or salty water, cheap red wine, or beer. (Cold tap water doesn't work because the wily things will just crawl out.) It may not quite fit in with your social schedule, but, honestly this really gets rid of any snail problem. Start in spring when your plants are tiny and at their most vulnerable. Simply pop the little horrors into the bowl so they drown. The first night, you'll catch 30, maybe 40. The second, the same again. But then you'll start noticing the numbers fall. All go into my red wine to die what I like to think is a convivial death, in a little cocktail party of doom.

Villain No. 2: cats

"My cats are no trouble in my vegetable beds," cat owners always boast. "That's because they're too busy ruining mine," you reply. Cats, those charming beasts, aren't stupid. They don't crap in their own backyard, but head over to the neighbor's where they powder their feline faces at leisure and dig up precious seedlings in the process.

When I redesigned my little city garden, I thought I was making six stylish raised beds. Apparently, I made six handy litter trays, the must-see destination of the feline world. My arugula was the first casualty, taking a direct hit from above that made the thought of a green salad distinctly unappealing. Since then, I've been close to tears on discovering a row of just emerged salad leaves strewn brutally all over the place, topped, charmingly, by cat doo-doo as if to add insult to injury. I swear all the neighborhood cats have been sent a memo informing them of a particularly immaculate public restroom. Spring is the real problem time for cats because of a double whammy: the garden tends to be fairly bare, with lots of patches of earth—cat-toilet heaven—and there are lots of vulnerable seedlings coming up just waiting for feline annihilation.

What do you do about it?

I've tried strewing citrus peel around (apparently they don't like the smell), but that didn't seem to work and made the garden look like a compost pile. Some people swear by ultrasonic scarers and lion poo, available from garden centers, which is supposed to frighten them. But, for me, there is only one real solution: sticks. Not to beat them with, but to lay across the beds, the twiggier the better. Holly branches are also good since no one—not even a cat—wants to squat over prickles. Keep any prunings from fruit bushes and trees and raspberry canes, the thornier the better, pick up sticks in the local park, or use bamboo canes if you don't have anything else, and create a crisscross tangle upon which no cat would dare to tread. And don't forget to cover pots too. If that fails, get a squirt gun.

Scallions (Salad Onions)

Snip them onto warm potatoes, salads, or into sandwiches, spruce up a tuna salad, or add to baked potato fillings . . . scallions (salad or spring onions) are super versatile in the kitchen and easy-peasy to grow. 'White Lisbon' or 'Spring Slim' are good varieties for both open ground and containers. A row of onions sown at the front of a window box and backed by lettuces and nasturtiums looks very perky.

Sowing scallions

When? Mid-spring to midsummer

In Pots

medium-sized container with drainage holes • all-purpose potting mix • onion seeds • 20 minutes

How? Add a layer of crocks to the bottom of the container and then fill it almost to the top with potting mix. Sprinkle the seeds thinly over the surface, then cover with a thin layer of mix. Water. Place in a sunny or partially shaded spot.

In Soil

pencil or stick • onion seeds • 10 minutes

How? Choose a sunny or partially shaded spot with well-cultivated soil. With your pencil or stick, scratch a shallow groove in the soil. Sprinkle the onion seed thinly along it, then cover with soil and water well.

What next? Keep moist. Investigate how big the onion bulbs have become, pull them up when you like the look of them and add them to salads.

Sugar Snap Peas and Snow Peas (Mangetout)

If you have an acre of kitchen garden and a legion of gardeners, by all means sow row upon row of regular peas and enjoy freshly podded peas all summer long. But if, like me, you have a small garden/patio, this isn't going to work. Peas take up space, they need supports, and they're fiddly to shell. And when you can buy cheap, delicious frozen ones that were ushered into the freezer within minutes of being picked, I really don't see the point.

But I do make an exception for sugar snaps and snow peas. You get to eat the whole pea, after all, and their sweetness and crunchiness when just picked are eye-opening. Eaten raw in salads or briefly stir-fried to tender but crunchy with a little garlic and ginger, they are exquisite. Try growing them in a hanging basket, a growing bag or container, or in soil. For an easy life, choose a dwarf variety and you won't have to provide much support for them to climb up. If you plant in a hanging basket, they will trail down. Good varieties are 'Sugar Snap' for a tall sugar snap; 'Sugar Rae,' 'Sugar Bon,' or 'Zucolla' for a dwarf sugar snap; and 'Dwarf Sweet Green' or 'Norli' for a dwarf snow pea. Or why grow green at all? Purple-podded peas are great eaten as snow pea (mangetout), and look amazing planted among sweet peas.

Sowing sugar snap peas and snow peas

When? Late spring to early summer.

In Pots

container at least 18 in. (45 cm) in diameter with drainage holes • all-purpose potting mix • stakes (such as old prunings, the twiggier the better) at least 16 in. (40 cm) long • sugar snap pea or snow pea seeds (a dwarf or compact variety) • 20 minutes

How? Push a handful of stakes into the potting mix, evenly spaced (unless you're planting in a hanging basket in which case no supports are needed). Push your seeds into the mix as far as the middle joint of your forefinger (about 2 in. [5 cm]) and about 2 in. (5 cm) apart. Water well and place in a sunny or partially shaded spot.

r A salad to put spring in your step

This simple salad makes the best of the first spring salad and vegetables ready in the edible garden. It's a celebration of the beginning of the growing season: baby fava (broad) beans, pea shoots, baby beets (beetroot), and tiny new potatoes may be small, but they're full of the sweetness and intense tastes of the new season.

Serves 3
8 or more small beets (beetroot)
20 or more baby new potatoes
3 handfuls of baby fava (broad) beans, podded
4 good handfuls of salad leaves
7 oz. (200 g) feta cheese, cubed
2 scallions (salad onions), roughly chopped
1 good handful of pea shoots
salad dressing

Wash the beets and twist off their tops, then roast in a medium oven for about half an hour or until they are soft when pierced with a knife. Alternatively, boil them until tender. Let cool. Wash the potatoes and then boil or steam them until cooked. Steam the fava beans for a couple of minutes and then peel them—they should pop out of their jackets easily. When the beets are cool, rub off the skins and cut them into quarters.

Wash and dry the salad leaves and place in a large bowl along with the feta, beets, fava beans, onions, and potatoes. Top with the pea shoots. Drizzle with salad dressing and toss well before serving with warm crusty bread, ideally while the potatoes are still warm.

In Soil

stakes at least 16 in. (40 cm) long (even longer for tall varieties) or an obelisk or trellis • sugar snap pea or snow pea seeds • 20 minutes

How? Spacing and depth of sowing as for pots, above. If sowing a dwarf variety, use stakes as support. If sowing a tall variety, either use extra-tall stakes or sow around the base of a tripod or trellis (you may need to provide extra support with string tied horizontally around the tripod in the early stages).

What next? If you want a constant supply of peas over the summer, resow when your seedlings are about 2 in. (5 cm) high. Keep the pea seedlings moist as they emerge. Snip off the pods and eat them whole about three months after sowing.
Where have I gone wrong? Powdery mildew is the main thing to look out for with peas.

Give pea (tips) a chance
Why not sow a pot of peas just for shoots? The tips of pea plants are a wonderful curiosity and delicious raw in salads, combining an unmistakable pea flavor with a fresh crunch. They'll be ready far before the actual peas. Sow as above and, when the plants are about 6 in. (15 cm) high, snip off the top pair of leaves at the top of their stems. They will resprout after a couple of weeks. Scatter the shoots on the top of salads, and see how long it takes your guests to guess what they are.

Pak Choi

Lush, leafy, and with a satisfying crunch, pak choi is surprisingly easy to grow. You can either harvest it as baby leaves 30 days after sowing—it's tasty raw in salads—or let the plants mature and steam them or add to stir-fries and soups. Group a container of pak choi with pots of oriental herbs and hot peppers for the ultimate outdoor Oriental larder. Sow again (or buy plants) in summer for leaves that will survive the coldest frosts. Good varieties include 'China Choi'; generally the green-stemmed cultivars are tastier than the white-stemmed ones.

Sowing pak choi

When? Late spring to late summer.

In Pots

large container with drainage holes • all-purpose potting mix • pak choi seeds • 20 minutes

How? Sow thinly ½ in. (1 cm) deep. Water. Place in a sunny or partially shaded spot.

In Soil

pencil or stick • pak choi seeds • 10 minutes

How? Choose a sunny or partially shaded spot with well-cultivated soil. With your pencil or stick, scratch a shallow groove in the soil. Sprinkle the pak choi seed along it (seed spacing as above), then cover with soil and water well.

What next? For baby leaves, thin to about 3 in. (7.5 cm) when seedlings are big enough to handle. Cut baby leaves after about 30 days, snipping above the smallest new leaf—the plant should resprout a couple of times. For mature plants, thin to 6 in. (15 cm) apart. Leave plants to mature if you want bigger leaves to steam or stir-fry.

Where have I gone wrong? Pak choi can suffer from flea beetle, aphids, caterpillars, root fly, and slugs and snails.

Edible Flowers

They're edible, not delicious. You wouldn't want a whole plate of these edible flowers, but as a garnish or sprinkled on top of a salad, they have a mild peppery taste and, more importantly, look absolutely breathtaking. They don't look half bad on the plant either.

Nasturtiums

Nasturtium flowers, with their upbeat bright yellow, orange, or red tones, are as prolific as the plants they come from. You only need two or three plants, and they'll sprawl heroically up obelisks and trellises and clamber in among other plants giving your garden a luscious air of colorful abandon and cottagey charm. My garden would be lost without them—they're great for covering bare earth and brightening up corners and love growing in containers as well as open ground. Choosing a form with variegated leaves gives them an even brighter look, or choose a dwarf form if you don't want it to climb all over the place. Sow seed directly into garden soil in a sunny spot from late spring to early summer or in pots inside from mid-spring on to get them off to an earlier start. Or buy ready-grown plants, then stand back and wait for the color explosion. Pick a handful and remove the stamens before throwing onto a mixed salad.

Borage

Borage is another plant perfect for the decorative edible garden. Its star-shaped blue flowers taste a bit like cucumber and are a traditional addition to Pimm's (see page 118). They also look very cool suspended in an ice cube, or add them at the last minute to white wine and see the blue flower turn

Nasturtiums

Borage

to pink. Either sow borage seed in mid-spring directly into garden soil in a sunny spot or buy a plant later in the season. It will sow itself once established so you only need to plant it once.

Viola tricolor (Heartsease, Johnny-jump-up)

Purple, mauve, and a yellow blushing throat, all small enough to fit into the palm of your hand. Sow inside in mid-spring in 3 in. (7.5 cm) pots on a sunny windowsill and then transplant outside to pots or garden soil when they're about 1 in. (3 cm) tall to a sunny or partially shaded position. Alternatively, plants are readily available from garden centers. Buy a tray of transplants and pack them into hanging baskets or containers. They'll flower right through autumn and winter if you regularly deadhead them. They look particularly nice growing among salad leaves.

Annual flowers such as nasturtiums freely self-seed, which means that seeds they drop at the end of the summer often germinate in the spring and pop up as brand new little plants. Don't pull them up; let them grow and save yourself the hassle of sowing new seed each spring.

Pot marigolds

Intense orange blooms and a reputation for attracting aphid-munching hoverflies have made pot marigolds (*Calendula officinalis*) a traditional kitchen garden favorite. They're also reputed to deter carrot fly since their smell is supposed to confuse the pests. The vivid orange petals look nice scattered on salads. Sow in late spring directly into garden soil in a sunny site or inside from early spring and transplant later.

Heartsease

Pot marigolds

Flowers Just Because

Yes, a lot of vegetables and fruit plants are pretty, but can they really compete with a forest of cosmos waving in the breeze or a wall of climbing sweet peas? Not only will these flowers bring in pollinating insects such as bees, but just as importantly, look amazing so you can lounge around with the Sunday papers, share a bottle of wine with a friend, or just waft about and not feel you're in a community garden.

Obviously, the list of flowers you can grow in your garden is as long as you want it to be, but these are a good beginning, easy to start from seed in early spring (or buy as plants later), cohabiting happily with fruits and veggies, and reliably flowering through to late summer, in some cases even late autumn.

Sweet peas

If you're going to have one type of flower in your edible garden, better make it sweet peas. These climbers have always grown cheek by jowl with vegetable and fruit plants. They're particularly good grown up the same teepees as runner and green (French) beans since they flower magnificently from early summer before the beans establish themselves. Their sweet scent is famous and their variously colored, lobed flowers are wonderful for cutting and bringing into the house. I put them in vases on the outside table too. The more you cut, the more flowers you get.

My favorites are 'Dorothy Eckford' (white), 'Cupani Original' (purple and the most strongly scented), 'Painted Lady' (bicolored pale and darker pink), and 'Black Knight' with its wonderful crimson black. You can buy them easily as plants in late spring, though sowing them is no hassle and quite fun since it's something to do in the otherwise sparse days of early spring.

Cosmos

I adore these daisy-like flowers, held on high stems above ferny foliage. They form a jungle in my garden every year, poking out through butternut squashes or tomatoes, or lolling languidly over strawberry plants. They paper over the cracks of the kitchen garden, filling dead space and bringing a sense of joyful color and abandon. I'd miss them if they weren't there.

A packet of Cosmos 'Sensation Mixed' will bring you flowers of white, light pink, and dark pink from early June to the end of October. Sow, barely covering with potting mix, in 3 in. (7.5 cm) pots on a sunny windowsill in mid-spring, two to a pot, and then thin to the strongest seedling when they are 1 in. (3 cm) tall. Plant out into the garden or large pots in late spring when they are about 6 in. (15 cm) tall. If they look leggy, pinch out the growing tip to encourage the side shoots to bush out. Plant at least 12 in. (30 cm) apart in a sunny spot in soil that has preferably had compost or well-rotted manure added. If planting in a pot, plant one to a 12 in. (30 cm) diameter pot. Throughout the summer keep cutting off the dead flowers to encourage new blooms to grow.

Nicotiana sylvestris

Cosmos

California poppies

Nicotiana sylvestris (Flowering tobacco)

These tobacco-plant giants bring a lush abundance to any garden, with their enormous, sweet-smelling leaves and trumpets of white flowers that gradually appear over the summer until they're looming over all inferior species. The fragrance of the flowers, particularly at night, is intoxicating.

Carefully sow these tiny seeds in a seed starting tray filled with potting mix on a sunny windowsill in early spring and then thin out to one plant per cell when the seedlings are big enough to handle. Transplant a seedling from its tray cell to a 3 in. (7.5 cm) pot when it swamps its tray and then into open ground when it swamps its pot.

California poppies

So intensely, upliftingly orange, these are quite simply feel-good flowers. The odd clump dotted around the borders or in pots will trail beautifully and spread around, attracting admiring stares, bees, and butterflies. Either sow directly into garden soil in late spring, or (more reliable in my experience) inside in a seed starting tray or small pots in mid-spring and transplant later. They will self-sow once established.

Climbers

Planting a climber to scramble up your fence or wall is great in an edible garden. Not only do they add structure and color year after year (most are perennial), but they bring in pollinating insects. The trellis fences of my tiny city garden play host to a white solanum, which flowers pretty much all year round, two honeysuckles, a jasmine, wisteria, and two types of clematis. They soften the borders and, so long as they are pruned so they don't take over the space, cohabit happily with fruit and vegetable plants.

Alliums

Try *Allium christophii* for a real firework of a flower, an enormous sherberty ball of star-shaped purple flowers on a tall stalk. Stunning. Plant bulbs in early autumn in pots or garden soil.

Dahlias

One of the most luscious flowers you can grow with blooms that come in all sorts of spectacular colors and shapes. My 'Bishop of Llandaff' with its deep crimson flowers and purplish leaves looks great when it gets into its stride in late summer. Plant tubers in spring or plants in summer. Traditionally, you're supposed to dig up the tubers and store them over winter, but I'm too lazy so leave them where they are, giving the plant a thick mulch of compost to protect the roots from frost in early winter. So far, it's come back every year.

Tulips

Plant bulbs in autumn in pots or garden soil. A sea of pure white tulips looks incredible poking above a bed of salad crops.

Tulips

Alliums

Dahlias

Figs

Typical conversation around a fig tree on a terrace somewhere in the north:

"Have you actually ever eaten any figs off your fig tree?"

"Of course I have."

"How many?"

"'Loads. At least ten."

"And you've had it for, what, three years?"

[Shrug]

It's lucky they look so exotic. It's also fortunate that, when you brush against them, their hand-shaped leaves release the heady, escapist scent of the subtropics. Lucky, because, when it comes to actually producing figs you can eat, these trees can be a little reluctant. Not when grown in a Mediterranean climate, of course—there they sprout out of church walls with reckless abandon. But if you live in a country where you can't rely on a long, hot summer and have winters that regularly dip below freezing, a fig tree might be best approached as a lovely ornamental with fruit bonuses rather than a reliable producer of pudding.

Having said that, a fig tree planted in a terracotta pot is a lovely thing, bringing a touch of exoticism to any garden, patio, or balcony. There are also things you can do to increase its productivity, so if you're prepared to put a bit of effort in, you will be rewarded.

The first thing is to choose a variety suited to your climate. 'Brown Turkey' is a popular choice with dark-red-fleshed fruits, although 'Brunswick' and 'Violetta' (which is particularly frost-resistant) are also good. Next, you need to restrict the roots by planting it in a container. This constrains the growth of the tree, which encourages fruit to form. Place the pot in a sunny, sheltered spot.

To have the very best chance of getting fruit, you also need to provide protection during winter. This is because next year's figs start off in the autumn as little buds and these are liable to die if subjected to very cold temperatures. Either bring your fig tree into a light, cool place such as a porch or conservatory before the first frosts or—less hassle—cover with a frost blanket. You can buy rather natty blankets or bags from many garden equipment suppliers, which are basically fleece hoods with drawstrings that you can place over your tree, keeping the whole thing snug. You remove these in spring when frosts are over.

Finally, it's a good idea to pinch back the growing shoots in early summer to divert the tree's energies into fruit production rather than putting out long branches.

If all that hasn't put you off, then you're in for a wonderful treat. Growing fig trees is a challenge, but the rewards,

when they do come (and they do, I promise), are truly worth it: sweet, fragrant, meltingly soft fruits eaten straight off the tree.

Planting fig trees

When? Mid-spring to late summer
Where? Outside in a pot

In Pots

container at least 18 in. (45 cm) in diameter • all-purpose potting mix • a fig tree, available from garden centers or online fruit suppliers (specialty fruit suppliers will provide the biggest range) • 30 minutes

How? Carefully ease your fig tree out of its nursery-grown pot and, with your fingers, tease out the roots a little if they look constricted. Then make a hole in the potting mix in the container and place the tree in it, covering with more potting mix so that the tree is planted at the same level it was before. Water in well and place in the sunniest, most sheltered position you can find.

What next? Keep the tree well watered and feed every couple of weeks with liquid seaweed.

Where have I gone wrong? Immature fruit dropping off could be a sign of inadequate watering—you may need to water every day in the height of summer.

Kale

I don't bother growing much of the brassica family, since they are, by and large, a magnet for pests and I don't want to cover my garden with anti-pigeon, anti-caterpillar netting and 24-hour surveillance cameras. I do, however, make an exception for kale, which I adore, not only for its hardiness, pest resistance, and earthy, good-for-you taste, but also its wide variety of leaves and colors, from the frilly terracotta red of 'Redbor' to the almost black, crepe-like plume of leaves of black Tuscan kale (also known as 'Nero di Toscana' or 'Cavolo Nero'). This is perhaps the hardiest one and my favorite. Others to recommend are the lush green 'Pentland Brig,' 'Dwarf Green Curled,' and 'Red Russian,' which has prolific, crunchy, pink-ribbed leaves. An exciting recent new addition has been "kalettes," a cross between Brussels sprouts and kale that thrives in small spaces and has dazzling purple ribbed leaves. Wait for the leaves to fall and then harvest the little side shoots that grow out from the main stem. Delicious sautéed or steamed.

The thing I love most of all about kale, though, is that it exists at all. When your garden gets ready to shut down for winter, the kales aren't getting the message. I love them for that brazenness—the fact that they remind you that life hasn't just stopped. They just keep on growing through the darkest, shortest days and producing lush leaves that are delicious steamed with plenty of butter and black pepper. They're also wonderful in soups with chorizo or borlotti beans. A winter roast isn't the same in our house these days without kale on the side. You'll be eating kale right up until mid-spring when the yellow flowers tower above the border, attracting pollinating bees to other flowers and crops around.

Sowing kale
When? Late spring
Where? On a sunny windowsill

In Seed Starting Trays

seed starting tray • all-purpose potting mix • kale seeds • 20 minutes

How? Almost fill the tray cells with potting mix and tap the tray down lightly on the table to settle the potting mix. Water from above with a watering can with a sprinkler attachment, then leave for a few minutes to drain. Sow one kale seed on the surface of each cell and then cover with a thin layer of potting mix.

What next? Keep your seedlings moist when they emerge. For planting out instructions, see Planting out seedlings, page 89.

Green curly kale.

r Kale and chorizo soup

In early spring, when nothing much is growing, kale is a bit of a rock star in the garden, shrugging off the gloom. It's one of those vegetables that tastes like it's doing really good things to you. Counteract all this health with some self-indulgent chorizo for a simple, tasty broth.

Serves 4
2 Tbsp. olive oil
1 large onion, chopped
3 garlic cloves, crushed
9 oz. (250 g) chorizo, sliced
2 pt. (1 L) chicken or vegetable stock
sea salt and freshly ground black pepper
3 large potatoes, peeled and cubed
7 oz. (200 g) kale

Heat the oil in a large saucepan. Add the onions, garlic, and chorizo, then cook for a few minutes until the onion is soft. Pour in the stock, season, and bring to boil. Add the potato cubes and simmer for ten minutes. Meanwhile, wash and finely slice the kale. Add to the pan and simmer for another five minutes. Serve in bowls with warm, crusty bread.

Herbs

Herbs come from hot, dry countries so are great for the distracted, busy, and forgetful gardener because they thrive on neglect. If you don't water them, they probably won't even notice.

I like having herbs in the garden because it makes me feel like I can cook. It saves you having to rush to the supermarket every time a recipe calls for a bunch of parsley or a few sprigs of thyme, buying packets you'll use half of and then leave in the fridge to turn to black slime (or maybe that's just me). I used to just buy those supermarket herbs in pots, but couldn't seem to keep them alive for more than a couple weeks, so now I either sow seeds or buy plants. Lots of herbs, such as rosemary, mint, thyme, and sage, last for years so only need planting once.

They're also some of the best-looking plants in the garden and smell gorgeous. A row of weathered terracotta pots containing rosemary, basil, and thyme looks the picture of elegance. Pop them by the back door and you won't even need to get your feet wet.

Here are some of the best-looking, best-tasting herbs to grow in a small space.

Basil

Basil can be sown directly into the containers you want to grow it in. Sow thinly and cover with a thin layer of potting mix in pots in mid-spring inside on a sunny windowsill. Alternatively, buy plants in spring/summer. When the basil germinates, keep it moist, but try not to water it in the evenings because basil hates going to bed with wet feet. When all fear of frosts is over, put your basil outside in a sunny, sheltered position. When the plant gets bigger, pinch out (and eat) the growing tips to encourage it to bush out. Pinch out the flowers when they appear. 'Sweet Genovese' is the one to choose for Italian-style mozzarella and tomato salads, pesto, and pasta sauces. Purple basil looks lush and gorgeous. For Thai cuisine, choose Thai (Horapha) basil. At the end of the summer, you can keep the plant going for a month or so by bringing it inside.

Cilantro (coriander)

Leafy and lush, cilantro (coriander) can be sown in medium-sized pots from early spring on a sunny windowsill inside or sown directly into the soil from mid-spring to midsummer in a sunny or partially shady spot. Sow thinly on the surface of all-purpose potting mix and barely cover. Or buy plants in spring/summer. When buying seed or plants, make sure you buy a variety that is suitable for leaf rather than seed production. Cilantro won't resprout once harvested, so you'll need to sow more than once to have a good supply throughout the summer. If it flowers, you can scatter them on salads or leave them to form seeds and use these fresh or pickled. Alternatively, leave the seeds to dry on the plant and then grind them in a pestle and mortar to add to stews, carrot and coriander soup, or vinaigrettes.

Oregano

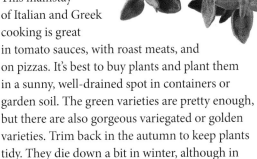

Is oregano the same as marjoram? I'm never quite sure. They taste the same to me. This mainstay of Italian and Greek cooking is great in tomato sauces, with roast meats, and on pizzas. It's best to buy plants and plant them in a sunny, well-drained spot in containers or garden soil. The green varieties are pretty enough, but there are also gorgeous variegated or golden varieties. Trim back in the autumn to keep plants tidy. They die down a bit in winter, although in mild areas you could still be picking leaves in the coldest months.

Chives

Either buy plants or sow a patch ½ in. (1 cm) deep outside in containers or garden soil in a sunny or partially shaded spot from late spring on. To harvest, snip leaves with scissors to within 1 in. (3 cm) of the soil level. The attractive, edible, pink pom-pom flowers look good on top of salads. It will die down in winter but should return year after year. Try digging up a portion in the autumn, potting it up, and placing on a sunny windowsill to have fresh chives throughout the winter.

The aniseedy ones

Tarragon

Delicious in a chicken salad, this subtly flavored plant has pretty, narrow leaves. It's not hardy in the cold so needs to be brought inside in the autumn. Buy plants, making sure you get French tarragon rather than the much less subtle Russian tarragon.

Fennel

With its delicate ferny leaves and impressive height, fennel strikes a dramatic pose in any edible garden. Herb (common) fennel (*Foeniculum vulgare*) is an easier plant to grow and rises up to almost 6½ ft. (2 m) so is great in the center of a bed. The stunning bronze form is a garden designer's dream. For how to grow Florence fennel, with its succulent white bulb, see Summer Jobs, page 94.

Chervil

A feathery herb that tastes really good with fava (broad) beans. Buy plants or sow in pots or garden soil from late spring on. It's also very hardy so another sowing in early autumn will keep you in leaves throughout winter.

Rosemary

Buy plants in spring and plant in a sunny, well-drained position. Rosemary hates being waterlogged, so if your soil is prone to being gummy, dig in some grit, pea gravel, or coarse sand. It does well in pots. Pick leaves as and when you want them—delicious added to the roasting pot with new potatoes and garlic or with lamb.

Thyme

Thyme is fairly easy to grow from seed, but takes a while to get going, so it's easier to buy plants. There are some gorgeous varieties out there, from common (garden) thyme (*Thymus vulgaris*) to deliciously scented lemon thyme and the variegated 'Silver Queen.' Thyme hates being waterlogged so plant in a sunny, well-drained spot in soil. It's happy in containers—a simple planting of thyme in a good terracotta pot with a mulch of pea gravel looks nice. Snip leaves as and when you want them, adding them to stocks, soups, marinades, and stews. After flowering, trim the plant into a tidy shape to keep it from becoming leggy.

Sage

Low-maintenance, handsome, and evergreen, sage looks good all year round. Fry in butter and add to pasta with Parmesan for a wonderfully easy supper. Buy plants in spring or summer and plant in a sunny, well-drained spot or pot. They'll be trailing over the edge in no time. Plants last several years. Purple sage is particularly pretty, though a bit wimpy compared to the green sort.

Bay

A bay tree in a nice terracotta pot is really elegant on a terrace or balcony. Bay is evergreen so looks good all year round and, because you only ever use one or two leaves at a time, you'll never exhaust the plant. Either leave plants to grow as bushes or prune off the side shoots to make a posh lollipop shape worthy of a classy Italian trattoria.

Parsley

Parsley can be very slow and fiddly to germinate so it's easier to buy plants that are readily available from mid-spring to summer. Choose from curly or French plain leaved and plant in a sunny or partially shaded position in moist soil. Parsley is very happy in containers and a row of the curly sort looks great as an edging. The curly sort is fantastically hardy over winter.

Sorrel

Intensely lemony, this little salad herb is great for adding a fresh tang to salads and also makes a sublime early spring soup. It's perennial so once established, it'll keep coming back with no work from you and it's one of the earliest plants in the garden to make its appearance. It doesn't mind a shady spot either. Sow from early spring to early autumn, or buy plants from mid-spring. Buckler leaf or French sorrel is best for salads, broad-leaved for soup. Or try blood-veined sorrel if you're feeling adventurous.

Mint

This must-have herb is a real bully, colonizing any bed you put it in. The traditional advice is to plant it in submerged pots in a garden border to stop it from taking over, but I tried this and the beast escaped within a season. So it's probably best in a fairly large pot. Mint is tolerant of shade, so is good for that tricky dark spot. It'll die down over winter but come back every year.

Where to start with varieties? For mint sauce, choose spearmint (traditional garden mint, *Mentha spicata*), Moroccan mint, or apple mint. For mint tea, go for Eastern (desert) mint or Moroccan mint. For mojito cocktails use spearmint. For the truly fancy, there's lime mint, orange mint, pineapple mint, or chocolate peppermint, which tastes like chocolate mint wafers. A few leaves with freshly picked strawberries are the business.

Lemon verbena

The scent of this herb is my favorite smell in all the world. It also makes the best herbal tea. Buy a plant in spring, plant in a pot, and put it in a sunny, sheltered position. Simply pull off five or six leaves and pour boiling water over for a lush, refreshing tea. After flowering, snip back the branches to a growing bud to keep the plant from becoming too leggy and in winter wrap it in a frost blanket or bring it inside to a cool, bright room and reduce watering to a minimum.

Herbal tea for three

I love making herbal tea from herbs in the garden. There's something so wonderfully simple about picking a few leaves, popping them in a cup, and covering with boiling water.

You will need

- 3 medium-sized pots with drainage holes, at least 8 in. (20 cm) in diameter
- all-purpose potting mix
- 1 chamomile plant—use Roman chamomile (*Chamaemelum nobile*)
- 1 lemon verbena plant
- 1 mint plant—any will make a nice cup of tea, but the following make the tastiest: spearmint (garden mint), Moroccan mint, Eastern (desert) mint, black peppermint
- 45 minutes

Add a layer of crocks to the bottom of the pots and then fill them almost halfway with potting mix. Make a small hollow in the center of the mix and plant one herb in each pot. Firm in with more mix and water well. Place in a sunny spot.

Chamomile tea is supposed to help fight a cold. It's also meant to have a calming effect so is one to drink before bed. Put three or four fresh chamomile flowers at the bottom of a cup and cover with boiling water for five minutes.

Mint helps the digestion so is good after a big meal or night out—put four or five leaves in a cup and pour boiling water. And there is no better way to end a good al fresco supper on a warm summer's evening than lemon verbena tea. It helps the digestion, has mild sedative properties, and an incredible zingy, lemon-sherbet scent.

Summer

Here Comes the Sun

Sauntering barefoot around the garden before work, gathering a handful of blueberries and raspberries to add to cereal. The scent of freshly picked sun-warmed tomatoes. Nasturtium flowers crawling among the scarlet beads of runner bean blossoms. The smoky promise of a barbecue. It's summer, and in the edible garden it doesn't get much better than this. It's about long balmy evenings outside with friends, drinking Pimm's filled with freshly picked mint leaves and strawberries, munching bruschetta laden with your own heavenly tomatoes and basil. In short, it's about the sun, the company, and most of all, the food.

Early summer is still busy—time to plant tomatoes, beans, zucchini (courgettes), cucumbers, eggplants (aubergines), sweet corn, and peppers. You can also continue sowing peas, beets (beetroot), salad, and carrots. But later in the summer brings a welcome time of laziness in the garden. The activity of spring is long over. The garden's slow decline to winter is safely far away. Pretty much all there is to do is water, feed your plants, and feed yourself. Popping outside for five minutes to pick zucchini, green (French) beans, strawberries, and raspberries for supper—straw hat and basket suitable, but not compulsory—certainly beats battling the supermarket aisles after work.

Whether you have a garden or a couple of windowsills, the outside larder is at its fullest. You could also be eating fava (broad) beans, carrots, herbs, lettuces, cucumbers, figs, tomatoes, chard, arugula (rocket), blueberries, peaches, plums, cherries, apricots, blackberries, garlic, beets, herbs, sugar snap peas, and towards the end, runner beans.

If you do only three things this season:

PLANT

tomatoes

PLANT

strawberries

SOW

green (French) or
runner beans

It could also be a riot of color out there—with cosmos, alliums, nasturtiums, dahlias, and climbers flowering their little hearts out among your crops.

Oh, and you're going on vacation and leaving all your crops to wither on the plant . . .

How to go on vacation and still come back to vegetables

Gardeners can't go on vacation. Ever. Or, at least, they can't unless they're prepared to come back to a garden they barely recognize. This is because, however nice your neighbors/extended family, no one will ever be able to water your precious garden like you can, let alone deadhead, tie in, prune, and generally hover over your plants with all the attention of a penguin standing on its egg

(admit it, you're obsessed). The universal crime committed by helpful vacation waterers is under-watering, particularly in containers. Bribe them with whole Camemberts, salamis, weekends in the Languedoc—anything to encourage them to water, and remind them before you go to particularly focus on window boxes, hanging baskets, and pots. Remember: they need watering even when it rains. A potted plant in full leaf is a very effective umbrella.

Alternatively, if you don't have any helpful neighbors or are so obsessive that you wouldn't trust them even if you did, you could buy an automatic watering system with a timer. These might sound horribly complicated, but are actually easy to set up and really take the hassle out of watering—whether your crops are in soil or pots—giving you the freedom to go away for the weekend or even long vacations without panicking about anything other than getting to the airport in time.

Tomatoes Part 2

When all risk of frost has passed—early summer is a safe bet—it's time to plant out your tomato seedlings that you started indoors in the spring.

In soil

Choose a sunny, sheltered spot in which the soil is well cultivated and has been enriched with compost or manure. The "sunny spot" part is important—to ripen sweetly, these southern hemisphere fruits really do need some heat.

By far the simplest way to support upright tomatoes is to plant them near a wall or fence and tie a length of string from the top of it. Twirl it around the stem of the plant a couple of times. Then, as it grows, twirl it round again every week or so—it's surprising how strong a support this is even for a mature plant heavy with fruit.

t Make new tomato plants for free

When you pinch out your **side shoots**, don't throw them away. If you push them gently into some all-purpose potting mix, they will root and become entirely new plants that will soon catch up with your original batch. This is a great way to increase your tomato crop.

Upright tomato plants can also look pretty growing up obelisks in the center of a bed. If you want to make it really look the business, cover the feet of the tomatoes and any bare soil with one or two nasturtium plants for a froth of orange and

Picking tomatoes

Of course, you can pick tomatoes any way you like, but the quickest and easiest way to harvest them without damaging them is **to push down** on the crooked "knuckle" of stem holding each tomato to the vine. This way you pick them complete with the calyx (green star bit on the top of the tomato) and avoid splitting the skin so they'll keep longer. It also makes a nice, clean little snap noise that I find strangely satisfying. But maybe that's just me.

yellow flowers or a zucchini (courgette) plant that will soon give a deep green sea of leaves.

In containers

Plant one bush tomato plant or three upright ones in a pot at least 12 in. (30 cm) in diameter, tied in to a teepee of bamboo canes. Three upright tomatoes are happy in a growing bag tied in to bamboo canes or supported by a string hanging down from the fence. Trailing forms and bush tomatoes such as 'Tumbling Tom' or 'Red Alert' will cascade beautifully over the side of a hanging basket or window box. Plant one plant in each hanging basket in all-purpose potting mix.

What next? Once little fruits start to appear, feed the plants every two weeks with tomato food or liquid seaweed. Upright tomato plants grow straight upwards with leaves and fruit coming directly off the main stem. However, they also tend to produce shoots in the joints between some of the leaves and the stem. If left to develop, these will sprawl all over the place and divert away energy that you need to be focused on the developing fruits and growing tip of the main stem. So you "pinch them out"—simply breaking them off between thumb and forefinger. Once you've got the hang of it, it's surprisingly satisfying and weirdly addictive . . .

Water your tomatoes often—perhaps every day at the height of summer. Those in growing bags and pots are particularly vulnerable to drying out. Once an entire truss of tomatoes has been harvested, remove the leaves below this truss. This discourages disease and lets the sun in. Once each plant has formed five trusses of tomatoes, pinch off the top of your plants one leaf above the top flower truss. This gives these trusses a chance to ripen before autumn sets in.

Where have I gone wrong? Tomatoes are relatively trouble free, but they can occasionally suffer from whitefly and aphid damage and then, later in the season, blossom end rot and blight.

Don't cry over split tomatoes

Early in the season, my tomato fruits usually get eaten before they make it into the kitchen. But if their skins are split, don't throw them away. Roast them in the oven with garlic and olive oil—the perfect sweet, tangy accompaniment for lamb or sausages. Mix them up with feta cheese, olive oil, olives, and thyme for a delicious Greek-style dish crying out to be mopped up with fresh French bread. Or simmer them with onions, garlic, and oregano for a delicious, simple pasta sauce.

Runner Beans

Look, I know what you're thinking. These are what granddads grow. Well, maybe they do. Runner beans are the archetypal crop of the traditional community garden (allotment), often seen growing next to an old man drinking nettle wine and wearing sandals over his socks. But let me try to rehabilitate this most misunderstood of vegetables. Yes, they're an old-fashioned favorite, and yes, you may have been given them as a child and thought they tasted like leather bookmarks because they'd been boiled for half an hour. But slice them into succulent ribbons using one of those handy bean slicers, steam or boil them for a few minutes, and top with butter, salt, and pepper, and I don't think there's anything I look forward to so much in my garden. Apart from tomatoes of course, but then tomatoes are in a league of their own.

Runner beans are perhaps the prettiest crop you can grow. With their bright scarlet flowers, heart-shaped leaves, dangling kipper-tie-like beans, and ability to climb in a picturesque fashion up teepees and obelisks, they're a must-have for anyone who wants looks as well as lunch. A single teepee will keep you in beans from midsummer right up to the first frosts. They're also at home in slight shade, so great for those who don't have entirely sunny gardens.

I'm a fan of 'Painted Lady' with its delicate red and white flowers, and 'Scarlet Emperor,' which has bright red flowers and very tasty and prolific pods. Other good varieties are 'Enorma' and 'Red Rum.' For planting in containers, 'Hestia' is particularly good since it grows only to about 20 in. (50 cm).

Sowing runner beans

When? Early summer

In Pots

medium to large, fairly deep container with drainage holes • all-purpose potting mix • a small obelisk or five bamboo canes • garden twine • runner bean seeds • 30 minutes

How? If you are sowing a climbing variety, either push your ready-made obelisk into the

t Never too late for beans

If you miss the boat and find your runner (or green) beans have become too mature, tough, and stringy to eat, don't forget you can eat the seeds inside. Simply take out the fresh seeds and **boil them** for 20 minutes as a side vegetable or to add to stews.

Runner and green (French) beans I harvested for the beans inside once the pods had gotten too tough.

potting mix or push in the bamboo canes in a rough circle and tie them together at the top. Push the seeds into the potting mix to a depth of about 2 in. (5 cm), one seed either side of each cane or upright support. If you've bought ready-grown plants, space them about 4 in. (10 cm) apart. Dwarf varieties need no supports, simply sow them about 4 in. (10 cm) apart (a 12 in. [30 cm] diameter pot would take five plants). Water. Place in a sunny or partially shaded spot.

In Soil

obelisk or five bamboo canes • garden twine • runner bean seeds • 30 minutes

How? Choose a sunny or partially shaded spot with well-cultivated soil that has preferably had manure or compost added the previous year. Somewhere out of the wind is ideal. Push your obelisk or bamboo canes into the soil as deep as you can, tying the canes together at the top, to prevent the wind blowing them over. For sowing instructions, see above.

What next? Keep a close eye out for slugs and snails at the early stages—they love baby runner

t Sweet companions

I often plant **sweet peas** at the base of the same teepee since they combine beautifully with the beans and flower much earlier so there's something nice to look at from early summer.

bean plants and can munch through a whole stem in one night. I can't count the number of times I've pondered over the reason for a limp-looking stem only to realize that it's been chopped cleanly through halfway down. Throughout the summer keep the beans well watered—particularly if growing in a container—and feed with liquid seaweed every three weeks or so. Once the plants reach the top of the teepee, pinch out the tops.
Where have I gone wrong? Apart from keeping an eye on slugs and snails, the only thing that tends to be a problem for runner beans is poor pollination. This is when you get loads of flowers but not many beans. This could be caused by not watering enough or cold and windy weather, which puts bees off their pollinating stride. When the weather improves, the number of beans usually does too.

Green (French) Beans

This is the bean of the classic Nicoise salad, otherwise known as "that bean in the cellophane packs flown in from thousands of miles away." We've all thrown these into our carts after a hard day and felt a little bit guilty about our carbon footprint. Grow your own and you'll gain significant air mile smug points. Chop the ends off, line them up like little soldiers, and wrap them in plastic wrap if it makes you happier.

Green beans make cool-looking plants, particularly striking in large pots or window boxes, where a mix of the purple, yellow, and green varieties together is very attractive. Choose a nice, sheltered spot for these tender creatures and only sow when summer has gotten into its stride. Climbing forms wind their way up canes, covered in little pink flowers, while the dwarf sorts form a dense, jungly mat of leaves.

Grow the climbing varieties, such as 'Blue Lake' and 'Cobra,' yellow 'Neckargold,' and purple 'Cosse Violette' up canes like runner beans. Or why not try 'Borlotti Lingua di Fuoco,' an Italian climbing bean with spectacular bright red and green-flecked pods? If you don't have the space, dwarf varieties such as 'Safari,' 'Tendergreen,' 'Purple Teepee,' and vivid yellow 'Rocquencourt' are all happy in pots where their heart-shaped leaves and clusters of dangling beans are bountiful summer itself.

Keep picking and they'll keep producing, but for a constant supply sow a handful of seeds every two weeks.

Sowing green beans

When? Early to late summer

In Pots

medium to large container with drainage holes • all-purpose potting mix • green bean seeds • an obelisk or 5 bamboo canes • garden twine (if a climbing variety) • 20 minutes

How? Sow as for runner beans, though you can sow them slightly closer together. A 12 in. (30 cm) diameter pot could take 6–8 plants.

In Soil

green bean seeds • an obelisk or five bamboo canes • garden twine (if a climbing variety) • 20 minutes

How? Sow as for runner beans, though green beans need a sunnier spot.

What next? As climbing varieties start to grow, twirl them round the canes to help them to cling on. Keep a close eye out for slugs and snails, and keep well watered, especially those in containers. Once the little beans start to form, feed biweekly with liquid seaweed.

Where have I gone wrong? Watch out for slugs and snails and black bean aphids.

 ## Beanfest in a box

Crunchy salad, beans, and glorious color all in the same box. You can use dwarf green (French) beans, but there's something deliciously striking about the purple ones. The dashing orange of the marigolds contrasts beautifully with the purple beans and bright green salad leaves. If you don't want to use a window box, all these plants will fit in an 18 in. (45 cm) diameter pot.

You will need
1 large window box with drainage holes, at least 2 ft. (60 cm) long and 8 in. (20 cm) deep all-purpose potting mix
3 dwarf green bean plants, preferably purple-podded such as 'Purple Teepee'
6 'Little Gem' lettuce seedlings
3 golden marigold plants such as *Calendula officinalis* (though any would be fine)
1 hour

Add a layer of crocks to the bottom of the box and then fill it almost to the top with potting mix. Plant the bean plants along the back and the marigolds in front of them, then fill the remaining space with the lettuce seedlings. Either wait for the lettuces to mature before cutting them or pick off leaves as and when you want them. Strew a few marigold petals on top of your salad for the height of homegrown elegance. Water well and deadhead the marigolds regularly to keep a supply of flowers.

Strawberries

An unfortunate, slug-related incident one summer left me with fewer strawberries than I had hoped for. This wouldn't normally matter, but I had some friends coming for lunch and had already bought the meringues and cream. I was forced to buy baskets of strawberries. From a store. It felt bad.

Later I mixed in the few berries that had escaped attack and asked my friends if they could tell the difference. They all promised that mine were somehow sweeter and better, but then, I was standing over them with a pruning saw.

There's something about growing your own strawberries that brings out the passion in people. Maybe it's because they're the archetypal summer fruit. Or maybe it's because there's something a bit decadent and sensual about eating a sun-warmed

t Don't drown me: the soil squeeze test

Strawberries will rot in sodden ground; a good test to see if you're overwatering is to squeeze a **handful of soil**. If water runs through your fingers, it's waterlogged. So lay off the watering for a while.

strawberry straight off the plant. My theory is that it's something to do with the seeds all being on the outside—there's nothing hard to watch out for in the middle.

You have to have strawberries in your edible garden, however tiny it is. Even if you only have space for a hook on an outside wall, it's worth planting a hanging basketful. You can pick them at the peak of juicy ripeness, unlike the store-bought ones, picked while still firm enough for boxing up and putting on a truck. Even a few plants can give you enough to smother in heavy cream, scatter on cereal, or turn into a mouthwatering smoothie.

The plants look cute, with scalloped leaves and daisy-like white and yellow flowers. I love the way the buttery, cushiony center of the flower gradually swells into the fruit. They're adaptable, too, growing as well in open ground as they do in pots, window boxes, and hanging baskets, where their fruits trail over the edges in a desultory way. A row of individual plants in small terracotta pots on a windowsill looks adorable. Or plant them at the front of a bed to make a cheerful border.

Different varieties of strawberries are ready at different times so, to get fruit over a long period, it's a good idea to plant a spread of different ones. For example, 'Gariguette' or 'Alice' yield in early summer, 'Cambridge Late Pine' in midsummer,

r | Barefoot breakfast smoothie

You wake up on a summer's weekday morning with half an hour to get yourself together and out of the house. Float outside, barely dressed, pick a handful of perfectly ripe strawberries and, within minutes, you are drinking an exquisitely refreshing, vitamin-packed smoothie that'll set you up for the day and still give you enough time to get to work on time. This recipe is so easy you can prepare it in five minutes. You can replace the strawberries with raspberries, blueberries, blackberries, or any mix of the above. You can't really go wrong—pretty much any combination tastes delicious.

Serves 1
4 large ice cubes
6 or more ripe strawberries
2 heaped Tbsp. Greek yogurt
1 Tbsp. runny honey
mint sprig, optional

Wrap the ice cubes in a clean towel and bash them with a rolling pin until they have become a fine snow (this is much less hard work than it sounds). Roughly chop the strawberries and put them in a bowl with the yogurt, crushed ice, and honey, then pulse it all up for a few seconds with a blender (a hand-held one is fine) until it's smooth. Taste and add more honey if it's not sweet enough.

If you're feeling decorative, add a halved strawberry on top. If you're really pushing the envelope for guests, you could even throw on a sprig of mint.

and 'Chelsea Pensioner' in late summer. Many plant suppliers sell helpful collections, which takes the hard work out of choosing. Alternatively, buy one of the "ever-bearing" or "perpetual" varieties, which will produce twice. These include 'Aromel,' 'Viva Rosa,' and 'Mara des Bois,' which combines the delicious aromatic taste of a wild (woodland) strawberry with the size of a cultivated one.

And don't forget the alpine or wild (woodland) strawberry. They may be tiny, but just a couple placed on top of a cake, for example, pack an intense taste way above their size, and you certainly won't find them in stores.

Planting strawberries

When? The usual time is late summer, for a crop the following year, though you can plant them in early autumn too. You usually buy plants with bare, spider-like roots that need to be planted out

t Never-ending strawberries

Strawberry plants are terribly accommodating. They not only produce lots of luscious fruit, but also make it super easy to raise the next generation. By midsummer you'll notice your plants putting out **"runners," basically baby plants** on the end of long stems. If you don't want extra plants, snip these long stems off close to the main plant. But if you do want to increase your number of strawberry plants next year, take a small pot and fill it with potting mix. Then place each baby plant, still attached to the runner, on top of the potting mix and tether it down with a piece of wire or pebble. After a couple of weeks, when the baby plant has rooted, you can snip it off. And, hey presto, you have a whole new plant that can be planted out in the ground in early autumn (space them about 12 in. [30 cm] apart) and will give you a nice crop of fruit next summer.

straightaway before they dry out, though you'll also see potted plants for sale, which are fine too. Alternatively, plant cold-stored runners (see right) in spring for a fast crop you'll be eating by summer.

In Pots

suitable container with drainage holes • all-purpose potting mix • strawberry plants • 45 minutes

How? Add a layer of crocks to the bottom of the container and then two-thirds fill it with potting mix. In window boxes and hanging baskets, it's a good idea to add a handful of water-retaining gel to the potting mix. Aim for three plants in a 12 in. (30 cm) diameter hanging basket or pot, or up to six plants in a growing bag. If you're using a terracotta pocket planter, plant as many plants as you have pockets, but do put a good layer of crocks in the bottom because the lower plants tend to get waterlogged in these traditional-style pots. In a window box, space them about 8 in. (20 cm) apart. Spread out the roots of the plants and lay them on the surface of the potting mix so they are not squashed, then fill with more potting mix. Water well and place in a sunny or partially shaded spot. They're woodland plants so will be OK in light shade, though a sunny spot will result in sweeter berries.

In Soil

strawberry plants • 45 minutes

How? Choose a sunny or partially shaded spot in well-cultivated soil, preferably to which compost or manure has been added. Make a hole for each plant about 12 in. (30 cm) apart and place the plant into it, spreading out the spider-like roots so that they aren't cramped. Firm in and water well.

Make sure you: Try to position the "crown" of the plant—the pointy part in the middle from where new leaves grow—so it sits on the surface of the soil. If you bury the crown, it has a tendency to rot. If you plant it too high, it might dry out.

t Strawberry takeout

The usual time to plant strawberries is summer, but **if you didn't do it last year, don't worry**. You can buy and plant them now. These plants have been held in cold storage and, when planted in the spring, will bear fruit 2–3 months later—just about as near in the fruit world as you'll ever get to a ready-to-go meal. If you planted strawberries last autumn, they should be flowering by now. When little fruits start to form, feed plants in containers with an organic liquid tomato or seaweed feed every two weeks.

What next? Keep moist as the plants become established. When little fruits start to form, feed plants in containers every two weeks with a liquid seaweed feed. At the end of the summer when the leaves turn yellow, cut them back to about 4 in. (10 cm) above the crown to keep them tidy and disease free over winter (except with "ever-bearing" varieties, which you can just leave as they are). You'll want to replace ground-grown plants every three years and container-grown plants every two, to keep getting a decent crop. This is no real hassle, since you can easily get new plants by rooting the runners.

Where have I gone wrong? Slugs and snails are your top enemies when it comes to strawberries. I swear they're telepathic. Again and again, I've had my eye on a perfect-looking fruit and thought I'll give that just one more day so it's really sweet. Invariably, the next day will dawn and I'll discover a snail or slug hole right in the middle. Be vigilant.

Summer Jobs 1: Planting Out Seedlings

Zucchini (courgettes)

Once all risk of frost has passed, it's safe to pop your zucchini plants out into their final growing positions. Choose a sunny spot with well-cultivated soil that has had manure or compost added. Plant climbing varieties at the base of obelisks or a trellised fence so you can tie them in as they grow. Give bush varieties a good 20 in. (50 cm) of space around them in garden borders so they can sprawl happily. Or plant compact varieties in large pots (one plant to a pot at least 18 in. [45 cm] in diameter) or growing bags (two per bag).

What next? Keep well watered and, once the first flowers appear, feed biweekly with liquid seaweed. Harvest the zucchini when they're about 4 in. (10 cm) long. Leave them too long and you'll be faced with a squash (marrow). And, believe me, nobody wants that. As I discovered to my cost one summer, there's only so many ways you can fill a "squash boat."

Where have I gone wrong? Zucchini are easy to grow, but problems could include slugs and snails and powdery mildew. Poor pollination, in which fruits start to grow but then rot from the ends, can also cause consternation if there is a cold, early summer when few pollinating insects are about. The good news is that the problem will improve when the weather does, but if you want to take a more proactive approach, try pollinating the flowers by hand (see page 88).

Cucumbers

Cucumbers are not quite as rampaging as zucchini, but they're still quite greedy, so if you're planting them in soil, choose a spot that has had manure or compost added to it. They need a sunny, sheltered position to feel happy. Plant two at the base of an obelisk and, when they have five or six leaves, pinch out the tips of the plants to encourage side shoots to grow. Tie these in to the obelisk. If growing in a pot, make sure it's at least 12 in. (30 cm) in diameter and grow up an obelisk, or plant two in a growing bag and tie in to bamboo canes. You could also try one plant in a hanging basket or deep window box and let the plant trail down rather than climb up.

What next? When the fruits appear, feed biweekly with liquid seaweed. Pick the cucumbers when they're no more than 5 in. (12 cm) long and peel them before eating.

Where have I gone wrong? Cucumbers suffer from the same ills as zucchini.

Hand pollinate for more pumpkins

In an ideal world, every baby zucchini, squash, or pumpkin would develop into a nice, big fruit. In a less-than-perfect summer, however, there might not be the number of bees around needed to pollinate the female flowers so they grow to a certain size, then rot and fall off. This is where you may need to lend a helping hand. **We're talking hand pollination, people.** I've updated the traditional tool for this job—a rabbit's tail—to a cotton wool ball since that's what I'm more likely to have in my bathroom cabinet. You could also use a soft brush like a makeup brush, but you'll get pollen in your foundation. Gently dab the cotton wool ball inside a male flower (one with a thin stem behind it), trying to get some pollen on the cotton wool. Then dab it inside a female flower (with the beginnings of a fruit swelling behind the bloom).

Squashes and pumpkins

Just one or two squash vines are enough for most small gardens or patios. Everything about these plants is big, especially their appetites. Choose a sunny, sheltered spot where the soil has been well cultivated and manure or compost added, and feed every couple of weeks with liquid seaweed when fruits appear.

Plant near a wall or fence and encourage them to climb up trellises by tying in the shoots as they grow. You could also plant one at the base of an obelisk or teepee and tie it up and around it to make an attractive focal point in the center of a bed or tub. Or just let them stretch out and sprawl in the sun. If you're planting in a container, choose a compact variety such as 'Baby Bear' and make it a big pot (at least 18 in. [45 cm] in diameter), or plant two in a growing bag.

What next? When the plants have five or six leaves, pinch out the growing tips to encourage side shoots to grow. For summer squashes such as 'Sunburst,' pick when they're about the size of an apple. Leave winter squashes and pumpkins on the plant until autumn.

Where have I gone wrong? Squashes and pumpkins suffer from the same ills as zucchini.

Eggplants (aubergines) and peppers

If you sowed these inside in mid-spring or have bought plants from a garden center, early summer is the time to plant them out. They do best in containers, but what kind is up to you. If you choose a window box, make it a large, deep one since they need a decent root run. If you choose a pot, make it no less than 10 in. (25 cm) in diameter for each plant. If a growing bag, cut three holes in the top and plant two eggplants or three pepper plants. If you don't plant a compact variety, you may need to provide bamboo canes to support plants as they grow.

Plant in all-purpose potting mix, water well, and place in the hottest, most sheltered spot in your garden. When the first little fruits start to form, feed the plants biweekly with liquid seaweed.

Kale

By midsummer it's time to plant out kale. Your borders are probably jostling with plants by now, but it's worth finding some room for these beautiful brassicas because they'll bring some welcome life come winter when the garden is looking bare. They grow into big plants so ideally need to be planted about 12 in. (30 cm) apart, but slot them in among other crops wherever you can. After all, by late autumn many crops will be removed, leaving the kales in splendid isolation. They like well-cultivated soil that has preferably had manure or compost added.

If your plants are destined for container growing, choose a pot at least 12 in. (30 cm) in diameter for each plant as they can grow very big. To beautify the base of the plant, why not sow some nasturtiums around the edges of the pot? Three or four transplants will be enough.

When planting them, firm them in well. The classic test is to pull the plant by a leaf. If the leaf tears before the plant is uprooted, you've planted it firmly enough.

Where have I gone wrong? Keep an eye out for slugs and snails, which can hide up in the leaf joints when the plant gets bigger, and caterpillars.

Sweet corn needs a grid (or a helping hand)

Hot, hot, hot, that's how these plants like it. So choose a prime position and plant them in a grid pattern. This is essential because otherwise, they won't be able to pollinate themselves properly (they rely on wind blowing the male tassels onto the female tufts of silk of neighboring plants below). Plant them about 18 in. (45 cm) apart each way.

If space is tight, you may not have enough sweet corn plants to ensure successful pollination and end up with empty ears of corn. To help them along, when the tassels look laden with pollen and the silks have formed, snip off a few anther-bearing tassels and touch them to the silks below to disperse the pollen. Do this every day while the tassels are full.

Watch out for slugs and snails, and keep the plants moist as they become established. When they get fairly tall, earth up the stems a bit to stabilize them against the wind.

Summery Salad Projects

P Salad with pep

This hanging basket looks very attractive, with the contrast of the green and red salad leaves and spiky clumps of arugula (rocket), and the purple and yellow violas tumbling over the sides add a sweet touch. Being up high, it'll be out of reach of slugs and snails.

You will need
- 1 plastic-lined hanging basket with drainage holes, at least 12 in. (30 cm) in diameter
- 1 handful of water-retaining gel
- all-purpose potting mix
- 3 'Green Salad Bowl' lettuce transplants
- 3 'Red Salad Bowl' lettuce transplants
- 5 Viola tricolor (Heartsease) transplants
- 6 wild arugula transplants
- 30 minutes

Add a handful of water-retaining gel to the potting mix before planting to cut down on watering (see page 18).

Fill the basket almost to the top with potting mix. Plant the lettuces, leaving a 2½ in. (6 cm) border clear around the edge. Then plant the viola and arugula transplants alternately around the edge. Firm in, water well and hang up in a sunny or partially shaded spot. Keep the potting mix moist.

Just reach up with scissors and snip off your leaves as and when you want them, then add a sprinkling of peppery viola flowers to the top of your salad for the final touch. If you snip the lettuce and arugula plants just above the smallest new leaf, they'll regrow several times.

P The classic

This classic salad collection is super easy to grow and always rises to the occasion. Two compact bush tomato plants, fragrant basil, and a row of lush oak-leaf lettuce will keep you in salad all summer. All you need is the dressing.

You will need
- 1 large window box with drainage holes
- all-purpose potting mix
- 2 bush tomato plants such as 'Red Alert' or 'Tumbling Tom'
- 1 'Sweet Genovese' basil plant
- 1 packet of 'Green Oak Leaf' lettuce seed (or any lettuce)
- 40 minutes

Add a layer of crocks to the bottom of the window box and then fill it almost to the top with potting mix. Making holes in the potting mix, plant the tomato plants at either end of the box and the basil in the middle, then sprinkle the lettuce seed thinly over any remaining space. Barely cover with a sprinkle of potting mix. Water well.

As the plants grow, keep the potting mix moist. Harvest the lettuce as baby leaves by cutting just above the smallest new leaf with scissors when the plants are about 4 in. (10 cm) high. Resow the lettuce when the plants stop growing strongly. Feed the tomato every two weeks with a tomato feed or liquid seaweed once fruits have started to form.

Radicchio

Added to milder-flavored salad leaves in autumn and winter, these crunchy, red, slightly bitter leaves are great—particularly good with blue cheese, poached pears, and walnuts. They're even better grilled, when their bitterness turns to sweetness (see page 147). In the garden, whether in pots or soil, they provide a welcome dash of color over the winter months, and an even more welcome harvest in early spring. As far as varieties go, 'Rosso di Treviso' is hard to beat, with deep burgundy leaves and striking white ribs.

Sowing radicchio
When? Midsummer

In Pots

medium to large container with drainage holes • all-purpose potting mix • radicchio seeds • 20 minutes

How? Sprinkle your seeds about 2 in. (5 cm) apart over the surface, then cover with a thin layer of potting mix. Water. Place in a sunny or partially shaded spot.

In Soil

pencil or stick • radicchio seeds • 10 minutes

How? With your pencil or stick, scratch a shallow groove in the soil. Sprinkle the radicchio seed along it about 2 in. (5 cm) apart, then cover with soil and water well.

What next? Keep moist. When the seedlings are big enough to handle, thin them to about 8 in. (20 cm) apart if growing in the ground. If growing in pots, thin to about six plants per 12 in. (30 cm) diameter pot. Harvest from autumn when the frosts turn the leaves from green to a rich burgundy color.

Where have I gone wrong? Radicchio doesn't tend to attract too many pests, but it doesn't like to be crowded. If you find your leaves turning brown and slimy, chances are they're too close together. Remove any slimy leaves, and thin seedlings to give them more space.

Artichokes

Architectural, stately, and downright huge, these plants look majestic at the back or center of a bed, rearing up above everything else. Somehow they make your garden look rather grand, no matter how tiny it is. Just a couple is enough for most town gardens, since a mature plant can take up 3 ft. (1 m) of your precious space and grow up to 6½ ft. (2 m) high (not one for containers, then). Expect up to 12 artichokes from each mature plant. Their spiny artichokes—actually flower buds that have yet to open—wave above long, beautiful, silvery-green serrated leaves. Buy ready-grown plants. They should last for a good few years.

'Green Globe' is a good variety to go for, though real show-offs might prefer the purple-headed 'Violetto di Chioggia.' Cut the heads while still small to eat whole or leave them to mature, then boil and eat them dipped in melted butter or mayonnaise. If you can bear to leave any on the plant, they'll reward you with beautiful, purple, thistle-like flowers.

Planting artichokes
When? Early summer to midsummer
Where? Outside in soil that has had plenty of compost or well-rotted manure added, in a sunny, sheltered spot. Artichokes hate being waterlogged so if you have a heavy clay soil, also add some gravel (grit) to improve the drainage.

In Soil

artichoke plant • 20 minutes

How? Dig a hole big enough for your artichoke plant, allowing a couple of feet around it for the plant to grow. Place the plant in the hole and then firm in, cover with soil, and water well.

What next? It feels a shame, I know, but to get a really strong plant, you should cut off all buds the plant produces in its first summer. From then on, harvest the buds when they reach a size you like eating. In the spring, mulch your plants with compost.

Where have I gone wrong? When your plants are young, watch out for slugs and snails. Feeble growth and rotting leaves in young plants are a sign of bad drainage—dig in some gravel (grit).

Blueberries

I'm sure it was the blueberry that saved me. It was a particularly bleak summer cold. My head was like achy cotton wool, my eyes sore, my nose streaming, and I couldn't face leaving the house to buy orange juice let alone acetaminophen (Paracetamol). Yet instinct drew me to the garden where I threw handfuls of blueberries into my mouth like a California vitamin junkie at breakfast. I swear I felt better by the end of the day (though six hours in front of the television may also have helped).

Blueberries have indeed been declared a superfood, packed with age-defying antioxidants, vitamin C, flavanoids, and even something that prevents the formation of wrinkles. I suspect they may be able to speak foreign languages. Even if they weren't such a wonder berry, though, I'd have a couple of bushes in the garden. They're so low maintenance you can ignore them all year and still get handsome foliage, delicate cream or pink flowers, and a crop of beautiful, sweet berries in return. They don't even take up much space.

I have three blueberries in my little garden, and they're up there with my favorite plants in the garden. They need no pruning apart from the removal of dead twigs, can be left outside all winter, and are largely untroubled by pests. 'Bluecrop,' 'Spartan,' and 'Earliblue' are all reliable, but the semi-evergreen ones, such as 'Sunshine Blue' and 'Toro' are the nicest looking because their leaves turn a stunning auburn in the autumn and brighten up the garden all winter.

Planting blueberries

Grow blueberries in a pot because they will only grow in ericaceous potting mix—available from all garden centers. Plant your blueberry bush in a container at least 12 in. (30 cm) in diameter in ericaceous potting mix and put it in a sunny position. Being acid-loving plants, blueberries should, strictly speaking, be watered with rainwater, not tap. But don't worry too much about this. I've always watered mine from the garden hose, and they've been laden with berries. From early summer on, when the flowers start to set fruit, give the bush a biweekly feed with a tomato feed or liquid seaweed.

Florence fennel

This aniseedy, succulent white bulb with feathery leaves is gorgeous sliced paper-thin and eaten raw in salads, or braised, but you really need to wait until midsummer to sow it because it has a nasty habit of bolting (running to seed) if temperatures drop. Choose Romanesco and sow directly into garden soil or pots ½ in. (1 cm) deep, then thin seedlings to 8 in. (20 cm) apart. Harvest in early autumn.

Pak choi

This oriental green is a fusspot about light and prone to bolting if sown in summer before Midsummer Day. But once that's over, it's well worth sowing a patch of pak choi either outside or in containers. It'll be a welcome source of lush, crunchy leafiness in the autumn and right up to midwinter when there's not much else around.

Just keep sowing!

My sturdy seed box.

Crops to sow every 2 weeks from March to September for a constant supply. Keep the seeds somewhere dry. I store them in a wooden box in alphabetical order – geeky, but it certainly saves time when you're trying to find a packet in a hurry!

- Beets (beetroot)
- Carrots
- Lettuce and other salad greens
- Peas
- Radishes
- Arugula (rocket)
- Scallions (spring onions)

Carrots sown two weeks apart showing successional sowing.

Fallen on chard times

You may already have sown the spinach-like 'Bright Lights,' Rainbow, or Swiss chard in the spring, but if you want to guarantee a welcome splash of color and lush greenery in the garden all the way through autumn and winter, sow in mid- to late summer too. Sow seed directly into garden soil or large containers for the patio and keep moist in the summer heat until established.

Summertime Essentials

How to water

I knew I had finally reached gardening obsession the other day while watching a police drama on TV. The suspect was watering flowers in his garden by sprinkling their petals with a watering can in the heat of the afternoon. "No," I all but yelled at the screen, "you're torturing them!" I can't remember whodunit in the end, but I know who was guilty of crimes against flowers.

Follow these watering tips and your plants will thank you for it:

- **Water the soil around the plants, not the plants themselves.** It's the roots that need water, not the leaves.
- **Water in the morning or evening on hot days.** If you water when the sun is shining, you can scorch the leaves and flowers. You'll also lose a lot through evaporation.
- **Soak the roots rather than just give them a vague sprinkle.** A few seconds with your thumb over the hose will barely wet the surface.

Plugging the gaps

So you've spent the spring sowing lovely seeds and now have a patio or garden full of growing plants, right? . . . Right? Sometimes life doesn't work out as we hope. Maybe you've been busy at work. Maybe you were on vacation. Or you just didn't get round to it. Just because you haven't been nurturing seedlings on your windowsill for the past month or so doesn't mean you can't have a garden full of burgeoning salad, herbs, vegetables, and fruit this summer. Garden centers and online plant companies have all manner of little plants available, ready-grown. They're a fantastically easy way to get your edible garden up and running over a weekend. They may not allow you quite the number

Bladderwrack Beach.

of varieties that you get when growing your own from seed, but the choice is improving every day. Cheating? Who's ever going to know?

Fertilizing: do I have to go to the beach now?

I keep mentioning "liquid seaweed" in this book. Before you think you need to head to the coast and fill a carrier bag with bladderwrack, let me explain that seaweed feed is available in bottles at any garden center and also online. All you have to do is put a capful in a watering can of water and pour it onto the soil around any fruit or vegetable plant. How often? It depends, but usually once every week or two (don't worry if you're not exact, plants don't have watches).

I used to mentally skim over the parts in gardening books that talked about feeding plants. It all sounded so technical, surely involving smelly powders and weird measuring equipment. But then I bought some tomato food from a store (the bottle

t How to read a fertilizer bottle

Standing in a garden center squinting at the back of a plastic bottle is trying at the best of times, but especially if you have no idea what you're looking for. Fertilizer labels can seem like a jumble of letters and numbers. Here's what it all means:

- **N** **Nitrogen:** for leafy growth

- **P** **Phosphorus:** for root and shoot growth

- **K** **Potassium:** for flower and fruit growth

The amounts that these chemicals are present in the fertilizer are then shown as the N-P-K ratio. For example, a fertilizer shown to be 20:20:20 would be a balanced feed, while a ratio of 10:12:24 would denote a high potassium feed such as that for feeding tomatoes.

Aim for organic feed and choose a balanced feed for all leafy crops and a high potassium feed for fruiting crops such as tomatoes and peppers.

DIY alternatives to bottle feeds

Comfrey
For tomatoes and other fruiting crops
A useful plant to grow if you have space. The plants have incredibly long taproots, so these draw up nutrients from the soil. The leaves, which are very low in fiber, can then be harvested up to four times a year. Lay them onto the surface of the compost where they will degrade, or add them to a bucket of water and leave them to decompose. The resulting liquid is high in potassium and can be used as a liquid plant feed when diluted to the color of weak tea.

Nettles
For leafy green crops
Get revenge on your stinging nettles by turning them into useful feed that is high in nitrogen. Cut a couple of armfuls of nettles, scrunch them up, and leave them in a bucket of water for two weeks. Dilute the liquid to the color of weak black tea, and water it onto your crops. Warning: it smells very strong!

had a big picture of tomatoes on it, it wasn't hard) and realized this feeding business is just a question of pouring a capful of dark brown stuff into a watering can and pouring it on.

If you don't feed your plants nothing terrible will happen. They won't die. But they won't produce so many tomatoes, hot peppers, zucchini (courgettes), or strawberries, the ones they do produce won't be as big, healthy, and tasty, and the plant won't produce for as long. Just get plant food that says it's for fruit or flowers; any that calls itself "tomato food" will do the job. I like liquid seaweed feeds because they're organic and they work. Also, I'm squeamish. There are all manner of ghoulish-sounding fertilizers out there. The Victorians used rotten fish mashed up with a spade. Old-timer gardeners swear by chicken poo or blood, fish, and bone. I think, on balance, you're getting off lightly with a very slight whiff of the seaside.

Supporting cool-looking climbers

Runner beans, sweet peas, squashes, green (French) beans, cucumbers, zucchini (courgettes), and peas can be a wonderful sight climbing up a teepee or clambering over a trellis or arch. Pop them in soil or in the center of pots on a balcony and you've got instant height. They're also a great way to grow a lot of crops in a small space.

Ready-made obelisks or teepees can be bought in garden centers and aren't expensive. All you do is push them into the ground and you're off. Or you can make them yourself by pushing five bamboo canes into the ground in a rough circle and tying them together at the top.

If you want a modern, urban look go for metal obelisks or maypole climbing frames, on which plants climb up strings pegged into the ground around a black steel pole.

For a looser, more cottage-garden style, choose willow or hazel obelisks. I leave mine in the ground all winter, since they look great even when they're bare.

Take tips from the cottage garden tradition

The cottage garden style developed in England from the traditional workers' cottages of generations past where limited funds and space meant flowers rubbed shoulders with fruit, herbs, and vegetable crops. Imagine a thatched cottage with a rose scrambling over the door, a picket fence, and a wiggly brick path leading through jumbles of flowers and teepees of runner beans. Chickens pecked around the plants, seed was saved to use year after year, and materials were recycled or handmade. In many ways the cottage garden is the inspiration for modern organic vegetable growing, making the most of the space we have while conserving resources and trying to avoid chemicals.

To help plants climb up fences or walls, it's a good idea to set up some trellising. It saves no end of fiddly tying in of wires and strings, since climbers will clamber up it with the ease of a Sherpa.

Arches are another quick and easy way to add height. You can buy fairly cheap willow and steel ones ready-made. Just push into the ground over a walkway, grow squashes, beans, and roses over them, and you've got an instant cottagey feature.

Whatever sort of structure you go for, make sure you push it into the ground securely before you plant anything, and choose a sheltered spot. It's easy to underestimate the weight of a teepee full of runner beans, especially when there's a wind blowing. I lost all my beans last summer when the teepee was toppled, ripping the poor things out at the roots. The scars still linger.

Mediterranean Veggie Combos

Patio-friendly Greek salad

Who doesn't love a Greek salad on a summer's day? Plant up these pots and recreate its classic mixture of juicy tomatoes, crunchy cucumber, lettuce, and oregano on your patio. All you'll need to buy are the feta cheese and black Kalamata olives.

You will need
- 2 large pots with drainage holes, at least 18 in. (45 cm) diameter
- all-purpose potting mix
- 1 small obelisk
- garden twine
- 2 cucumber plants—an outdoor variety such as 'Burpless Tasty Green'
- 7 or more lettuce seedlings—a mini romaine (cos) type such as 'Little Gem' or 'Pinokkio'
- 1 packet of scallion (salad or spring onion) seeds such as 'White Lisbon'
- 2 bush tomato plants such as 'Red Alert' or 'Tumbling Tom'
- 1 Greek oregano plant
- 1 hour

Add a layer of crocks to the bottom of both pots and almost fill them with potting mix. In one pot, push the obelisk into the middle, then plant the cucumber plants on either side of it, loosely tying the stems to the frame. Plant your lettuce seedlings around the edge of the pot about 6 in. (15 cm) apart in any remaining space. Then sprinkle a pinch of spring onion (scallion) seeds into the gaps between the lettuces and barely cover with potting mix. In the other pot, plant the tomato plants and oregano. Firm all the plants in and water well.

Water regularly and feed every two weeks with liquid seaweed. When the onion seedlings are big enough to handle, thin them to about 1 in. (3 cm) apart, eating the thinnings. When the cucumber plants have five or six leaves, pinch out the growing tip to encourage side shoots to grow and tie these in to the obelisk. When fruits appear on the cucumber and tomatoes, feed biweekly with liquid seaweed.

Ratatouille riot

Bring the flavors of Provence to your patio with this rambunctious collection of big, hearty Mediterranean heat lovers. Give these tomatoes, zucchini (courgettes), eggplants (aubergines), peppers, and oregano a sun-drenched spot, and you could be recreating the classic French stew by late summer.

You will need
 2 large containers with drainage holes—old wooden wine crates are ideal,
   or divide your plants between 2 large pots at least 18 in. (45 cm) in diameter
   or 2 large window boxes at least 2½ ft. (80 cm) long
 all-purpose potting mix
 1 bush tomato plant—a tumbling variety such as 'Tumbling Tom'
 1 eggplant (aubergine) plant—a dwarf baby variety such as 'Ophelia' or 'Orlando'
 1 sweet pepper plant—a dwarf variety such as 'Redskin'
 1 zucchini (courgette) plant—a compact variety such as 'Tuscany' or 'Defender'
 1 thyme plant
 40 minutes

   Add a layer of crocks to the bottom of your containers and half fill them with potting mix. Arrange the plants on the potting mix as you want them, remembering to allow room for the tomato and zucchini to trail, then fill the containers almost to the top, firming the plants in well. Water well. Place in a sunny position and feed every two weeks with tomato feed or liquid seaweed.

Lemons

Growing lemon trees is a favorite pastime of mine. I say "growing lemon trees" rather than "growing lemons" because, in truth, the actual harvest I've had from my citrus charge over the years could be described as, well, slim. But I'm hooked on the things. I fuss around my ten-year-old tree like a midwife, feeding it with its special feed, misting its leaves, and admiring its flowers and tiny green lemons with a look of wonder. I've been known to remove scale insects from its leaves with my hands and squash them between my fingers. And all because of that fantasy of sitting in my garden on a warm summer's day, the scent of citrus blossom on the air, sipping a glass of gin and tonic with a slice of my own lemon jostling with the ice cubes—a scenario that has, if I'm honest, only happened one time. Yes, growing lemon trees in a less-than-Mediterranean climate is a challenge.

Traditionally, lemon trees have been grown in conservatories, or at least brought inside into one for the winter. But these days, varieties such as 'Eureka' boast of being able to stay outside all year round. Certainly, my Meyer lemon has always survived uncovered, but you'd probably get a better crop if you gave your tree a frost blanket (see page 147) over the coldest months.

Lemons are needy. There is special food available from good nurseries—one for summer, one for winter. How high maintenance is that? They'll need the warmest, most sheltered spot on your terrace and also need to be planted in very free-draining soil—a potting mix with lots of perlite or gravel (grit). They're fussy about watering, liking a good drenching now and then rather than little and often. Oh, and did I mention they prefer rainwater to tap? If they were a person, they'd be a Victorian maiden, prone to fainting spells and constantly needing her corset loosened.

So why do I persist in growing lemon trees and, more to the point, why am I recommending you do? Because they're beautiful trees—they look exotic with their glossy evergreen leaves and heavenly scented flowers—because they're a bit different, and because, you never know, one day you might be able to reach out from your dining chair and nonchalantly pick a perfect lemon and slice it into the glasses of your impressed guests.

Other than the above varieties, other recommended lemons include 'La Valette' and 'Quatre Saisons.'

Planting lemons

Bought lemon trees can usually stay in the pot they came in for a season. Repot the following spring into a slightly larger pot filled with potting mix along with a good few trowelfuls of gravel (grit). Keep your tree in a sunny, sheltered spot on the terrace. **Where have I gone wrong?** Watch for scale insects and red spider mites.

What to Do with All These Herbs? Part 1

r Homegrown pesto sauce

Use your own freshly picked basil leaves and even your own garlic in this great, quick lunch full of the flavors of summer.

Serves 2
- 1 handful of pine nuts
- 6 Tbsp. roughly chopped, freshly picked basil leaves
- ½ garlic clove
- 1 handful of freshly grated Parmesan cheese
- olive oil
- sea salt and ground black pepper

Lightly toast the pine nuts in a dry frying pan for 2–3 minutes. Blend them in a processor with the basil, garlic, and Parmesan. Slowly blend in olive oil in stages until it's a thick, gloopy consistency. Season to taste. Stir the sauce into cooked and drained hot pasta and sprinkle with more Parmesan if you like.

r Herb butter

Your herbs should be going great guns by midsummer, but by autumn some of them, such as chives and tarragon, will be running out of steam. Preserve summer by making delicious herb butters that can be sliced directly from the freezer and added to the top of steaks and vegetables in winter.

Makes 6 portions
- 1 handful of any soft green herb, such as parsley, tarragon, or chives, chopped
- 6 oz. (175 g) soft butter
- 1 Tbsp. lemon juice

Beat the butter in a bowl until creamed. Add the herbs and lemon juice. Then place the herby butter on plastic wrap and roll it into a sausage shape. Put it in the freezer. When you want to use it, simply cut slices of butter as required, rewrap the rest with plastic wrap, and return to the freezer.

Frozen herb cubes

It's a great idea to freeze your herbs in their prime in ice-cube trays so you can enjoy your own fresh herbs all winter. Simply cut some, wash them, chop them up, and add them to your ice cube tray, then fill with water and freeze. You can then either defrost the cube to use the herbs or, as I do, just chuck them frozen into casseroles or sauces and watch them melt, releasing their freshly cut flavor even in the depths of winter.

Summer Jobs 3: Tidying Up

Figure to prune early

When? Early summer

That high-maintenance specimen the fig tree needs a little attention in early summer. The new shoots should be growing well by now but you don't want the tree to put all its energy into growing long shoots; you want it to plump up those tiny, new fig fruit buds. So pinch out each new shoot so that only five leaves remain. You should be able to do this with your thumb and forefinger.

Fewer plums now, more plums later

When? Midsummer

Plums are such pleasers—they produce far too many plums and then exhaust themselves so much they don't produce anything the following year. Do them a favor by thinning the fruit in midsummer so you are left with one plum every 2 in. (5 cm). It's agony to throw away healthy fruit, I know, but it's better than having no plums next year.

Maximize your mint

When? Midsummer

Give mint a haircut in midsummer when it's starting to look a bit rough, cutting the stems back halfway to just above a bud. It will produce pretty, delicate new leaves for autumn. And, if you want fresh leaves throughout winter, dig up a portion of root in autumn, put it in a pot with fresh potting mix, and place on a sunny windowsill. You could be fighting your hangover with fresh mint tea on New Year's Day.

A tight fit for peaches

When? Midsummer

A peach ripening against a warm wall is a wonderful thing. You return to it daily to see how the red blush spreads over the creamy skin and it softens to an aromatic ripeness. Unfortunately, someone else is also watching. The birds . . . And the squirrels . . . And the mice. If you don't want to discover a half-gnawed peach on one of your inspections, better take precautions, and what better than hosiery?

Cut off the feet and put them over each individual peach. The critters will stay away.

Keep raspberries close

When? Midsummer

If you have autumn-fruiting raspberry canes, they'll be getting tall and a bit sprawling by now. Push in some bamboo canes and tie the raspberry canes to them to keep the bush neat. Also keep an eye out for errant new canes—raspberries love to colonize new areas—and dig up any that have strayed too far from the original bush with a hand trowel and compost them.

Rollercoaster berries

When? Midsummer

If you're growing a blackberry against a wall or fence, it will be sending out long, loopy shoots by summer. Loop them up and down like a rollercoaster on one side of the base, tying them into parallel wires.

Summer Jobs 4: Harvesting

Garlic: the dig test

When? Early summer

Depending on the variety, any garlic that you planted in autumn will be ready to harvest from late spring (for example, 'Early Wight') to midsummer (for example, 'Albigensian Wight'). Keep an eye on the leaves, and when they start to turn yellow have an experimental digging expedition to see how big the bulbs have become. If they're still small, keep them well watered to help swell and have another look in a week or so.

If you're happy with the size of the bulbs, carefully dig up the bulb with a trowel, leaves and all. If it is a hardneck or short-storing variety, such as 'Early Wight' or 'Purple Wight,' you'll want to use your garlic fresh, so simply use it as you wish (it makes a glorious chicken and very garlicky soup). For longer-storing varieties, hang the bulbs up by the leaves somewhere warm and dry. After about three weeks, when the leaves rustle and the skin of the bulbs has turned papery, they are ready to store. This is when you locate your inner medieval French peasant and braid (plait) the leaves together. If, like me, that is beyond your weaving skills, just loosely tie the leaves together and hang your bunch of garlic up in the kitchen within reach of a chopping board. It should keep for months, during which time friends will gaze admiringly at your homegrown harvest and say "Wow, did you grow all that?" to which the correct response is to nod modestly.

Sweet corn: the fingernail test

When? Late summer

By late summer, your cobs should be bulging out from the sides of your sweet corn plants. I say "should" because this is not the most reliable of crops in a changing climate. Now you have to pick it just at the right moment.

I always get a bit anxious about timing the ripeness of sweet corn because traditional advice makes it all sound rather critical. When the silks—the hair-like fronds coming out of the cob—start turning dark brown, they say, pull back the husk of the cob and jab your fingernail into one of the kernels. If the liquid is watery, it's still unripe. If it's doughy, it's overripe. If it's milky, it's just perfect. You'd think you were landing a big airplane on a short runway, not picking a vegetable.

Is it safe to pop out to the stores, I wonder, or will I come back and find, God forbid, I've gone straight from watery to doughy and missed milky altogether? But maybe you're not such a natural worrier. Good luck with it anyway.

Turn Up the Heat

Salsa in a box

Here's one for fajita fans. Grow this collection of sweet, succulent tomatoes and crunchy lettuce, onions, fiery hot peppers, and cilantro (coriander) for fresh, delicious fillings for Mexican classics such as tacos and burritos. If you don't want to use a window box, divide the plants between a couple large (at least 18 in. [45 cm] diameter pots) instead.

You will need
1 large window box with drainage holes, at least 2½ ft. (80 cm) long and as deep as possible
all-purpose potting mix
2 bush tomato plants such as 'Red Alert' or 'Tumbling Tom'
1 hot pepper plant—any dwarf or container variety such as 'Etna'
1 cilantro (coriander) plant
5–6 lettuce seedlings—a small, crunchy variety such as 'Little Gem' is ideal
scallion (salad onion) seed such as 'White Lisbon'
40 minutes

Add a layer of crocks to the bottom of the box and two-thirds fill with potting mix. Making small holes in the potting mix, plant the tomatoes and hot peppers at the back, with the tomatoes in the corners and pepper in the middle. Fill with potting mix so the plants are at the same level as they were in their pots. Plant the cilantro in one of the front corners and then the lettuce seedlings along the front of the box about 6 in. (15 cm) apart. Finally, sprinkle a pinch of scallion seeds in each of the gaps between the lettuces. Cover thinly with potting mix. Water well and place on a sunny windowsill.

When the scallion seedlings are big enough to handle, thin so they are about 1 in. (3 cm) apart (eat the thinnings in salad, they're delicious). Keep the box well watered and feed it every couple of weeks with liquid seaweed. Resow the scallions and replant the lettuce and cilantro if needed to keep a constant supply throughout the summer. Leave the tomato plants to trail over the sides.

Thai for two

Relishing the thought of recreating that pad thai you had at that spot downtown you like? Here's all you need to bring the flavors of Bangkok to soups, stir-fries, or curries. Line up cilantro (coriander), mulberry-edged Thai basil, a plume of fragrant lemongrass, and a glossy hot pepper plant for that important blast of heat. Finish it all off with a pot of crunchy pak choi. Rather than cram all these plants in a window box, they'll benefit from being in separate pots so these could just as easily be arranged on a patio or balcony.

You will need
  4 pots with drainage holes, at least 8 in. (20 cm) in diameter
  1 pot with drainage holes, at least 18 in. (45 cm) in diameter
  all-purpose potting mix
  4 pak choi plants
  1 hot pepper pepper plant suitable for container growing, such as
    'Etna.' If you were being strictly Thai, you would grow Thai
    bird's eye pepper, but any compact variety will do
  1 pot of Thai basil (*Ocimum basilicum* 'Horapha Nanum')
  1 lemongrass plant
  1 pot of cilantro (coriander)
  30 minutes

  Add a layer of crocks to the bottom of the pots and then fill them almost to the top with potting mix. Transplant the pak choi plants into the larger pot, firm in well, and water. Then transplant the pepper, basil, lemongrass, and cilantro into the remaining pots. Place them on a sunny windowsill or patio and water well.

  Pinch out the growing tips of the basil (and eat them) from early summer onwards to encourage it to bush up. Resow or replant the cilantro when needed—it's a short-lived plant and doesn't resprout when the leaves are cut. Feed the pepper weekly with a high-potash feed such as liquid seaweed when it starts to fruit. In autumn, bring it and the lemongrass inside to a sunny windowsill so that the peppers can fully ripen and the lemongrass can survive the winter.

Entertaining

CALL IT INADEQUACY or rampant perfectionism, but cooking for more than two guests fills me with intense performance anxiety. Will the gravy taste like anything but stock powder? Will I unintentionally purée the broccoli again? Transfer the whole caboodle outside, however, and I magically transform into chef extraordinaire, anticipating hordes of hungry guests with nothing but pleasure, like a bargain-price Martha Stewart. What is it about eating outside that brings out the carefree in even the most hopeless of hosts? Usually a slave to a recipe, I only need a whiff of an al fresco grill and I'm throwing salads, marinades, and impromptu puddings together with happy abandon. And if a couple of sausages fall through the barbecue grill and turn to charcoal, who cares?

Let's Go Outside

It's like when you were at school and the teacher said, "It's too hot, we're going to work outside today," which, as everyone knew, was a signal to gossip, draw on your hands in pen, and daydream to the hazy backdrop of someone mowing grass. It's the same when eating outside. Normal rules don't apply. People get up halfway through their meal to poke the grill. Everyone's in and out of the kitchen carrying bowls. Someone's dropped the potato salad in the dahlias. No one is paying so much attention to the food because it shares double billing with the sunshine and general charm (you hope) of your surroundings. But, if they were, it wouldn't matter, because, as everyone knows, food tastes better when you eat it outside. And when that food includes tomatoes, herbs, garlic, new potatoes, peppers, zucchini (courgettes), and strawberries that you've just picked feet away from the table, it tastes better than ever.

r Farm to table to wow

Follow these references to seasonal recipes throughout the book:

Dishes
- Cinnamon apple crisps — 142
- Corn on the cob — opp. page
- Crisp raspberry and cream stacks — 137
- A decadent winter salad — 146
- Kale and chorizo soup — 69
- Quick, easy, and delicious bruschetta — 119
- A salad to put spring in your step — 60
- Speedy squash — 132

Drinks
- Barefoot breakfast smoothie — 84
- A fruitful Pimm's — 118
- Herbal tea — 73, 115
- A mojito to banish a day at the office — 118

Toppings
- Herb butter — 104
- Homegrown pesto sauce — 104
- The very freshest tzatziki — 119

New (salad) blue potatoes cut up for roasting.

So how do you make your outside dining experience as glorious as possible? A little attention to outside lighting, seating, and decoration can turn even the most humdrum of balconies or terraces into twinkling, magical wonderlands you won't want to leave until the wee hours of the morning. Tear herbs and throw them right into salads after a quick rinse under the garden faucet. Eat strawberries straight from the plant after a quick dip in some whipped cream. After all, where better to enjoy the fruits of your labors but in their natural setting?

The Barbecue

r Corn on the cob

Barbecuing is not a science requiring a post-grad degree, starched chef's hat, and gleaming set of different-sized tongs, despite what some may tell you. It's a question of lighting the corner of a paper bag and walking away, then coming back about half an hour later with an herby lamb chop or steak. Barbecues have moved on from the old days when people fiddled around with charcoal that never seemed to light until all the guests were so drunk they had to go home.

For we now have "instant lighting" charcoal that comes in its own handy paper bag. So wondrous is this product that you don't even have to touch the charcoal, just light the corner of the bag with

Sweet corn is not the easiest crop to grow in a northern climate. But if you get it right, you're in for a real treat on barbecue night. In fact, I'd go so far as to say it's worth scheduling a barbecue entirely around your sweet corn harvest, so delicious is it when freshly roasted on the grill. Simply pull a cob off the plant, husks, silks, and all, and submerge in cold water for at least an hour. Shake to drain and then place on the grill for 20 minutes, turning occasionally. Remove the husk and silk before eating with plenty of butter, salt, and freshly ground black pepper.

a match and the whole thing slumps to perfect, cookable-on embers.

These days you can buy pretty stylish barbecue sets, too: little silver, blue, or pink numbers so cute you want to pat them. Or braziers (I'm currently in love with mine) that cook a steak beautifully, but that you can also burn logs in. Sit around it, toast marshmallows, and warm your hands when the night turns chilly. And don't knock those disposable foil barbecue sets you can get in supermarkets. Despite what barbecue snobs may say, they work just fine and you won't even have to clean the grill pan afterwards.

More homegrown al fresco gorgeousness

There are lots of ways a barbecue can make the most of your freshly picked fruit and vegetables. How about shish kebabs of zucchini (courgette), sweet pepper, onion, eggplant (aubergine), and halloumi cheese? A warm salad of just-dug new potatoes and fava (broad) beans? Or baby beets (beetroot) roasted in foil served with a thick dip of crème fraîche and chives? For pudding, there might be raspberries, strawberries, or blueberries. For the easiest dish, throw them onto store-bought meringues with heavy whipping cream. Or, if you're feeling a bit more fancy, sandwich them between layers of crisp phyllo pastry and whipped cream.

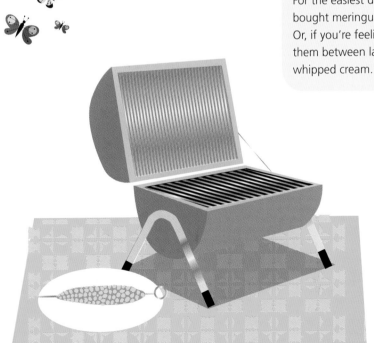

What to Do with All These Herbs? Part 2

On the grill
Throw twigs of fresh rosemary or thyme onto the barbecue embers and fill the air with a delectable herby scent. The oils will flavor the food, too.

In marinades
Garden herbs are fantastic for making marinades for barbecue meats. They can transform a steak or lamb chop into something delectable in an hour. Woody, robust herbs such as thyme, oregano, and rosemary when mixed with garlic, lemon juice, and olive oil are always a winner. Rosemary goes particularly well with lamb, thyme with chicken, and oregano with grilled halloumi cheese or tofu for your vegetarian guests. All these herbs are easily grown in pots. Use a mortar and pestle to bash the woody herbs up a bit to release their oils. Lay your barbecue meat in the mixture in a bowl for at least an hour—overnight gives a real chance for the flavors to penetrate—and then put it on the grill.

In salads
Other, less woody herbs such as parsley, cilantro, basil, mint, chervil, and chives are worth their weight in gold too. Tomato salad is an adaptable beast—when eaten with basil it tastes totally different to the way it does with cilantro or parsley. Try mixing up red and orange cherry tomatoes, topped with buffalo mozzarella and torn basil. Mint leaves are delicious with fresh peas, baby fava (broad) beans, or warm, freshly dug new potatoes, and a potato salad just isn't the same without a generous handful of chopped chives.

For the morning after
Over-indulged the night before? Relocate your inner peace and clear your head with some herbal brews. Try putting five or six rosemary leaves in the bottom of a cup and pouring in boiling water. Leave for a few minutes and then drink. A lemon verbena tea will also banish the cobwebs. Pour boiling water over five or six leaves and set aside for a few minutes before drinking—preferably in a dark room. If this still doesn't work, make yourself a bacon sandwich and take an acetaminophen.

The Garden: Setting Up with Style

Any outside space can be transformed into a den of dining awesomeness. The only thing that really matters is that you feel comfortable. After all, you're not going to have a rip-roaring evening if your guests' buttocks have gone to sleep on a cast-iron filigree chair, however elegant it is. I've had perfect evenings lounging on cushions on a rug with tiki torches (garden flares) pushed into pots nearby as light. So dégagé was the scene that a guitar may even have been produced at some point, about which probably the less said the better.

Furniture-wise, I always think lightweight is best so you're not restricted to one place. Bistro-style sets—round metal folding tables and wooden slatted chairs—are cheap, stylishly simple, and can be left outside all winter. Ugly plastic tables can be covered with throws or tablecloths and chairs

t Here's one I grew earlier . . .

It's not that you're a show-off, of course, but really what is the point in growing a lemon or fig tree if your guests can't be suitably impressed by their fragrant exoticism and your obvious gardening know-how? So make sure they're near the table. The scent of citrus blossom is particularly tropical, especially if you haven't masked it with the whiff of burning lamb chops. And if you have actually managed to grow a lemon, this would be the time to pick it, slice it, and add it to gin and tonic. As for a fig tree, a potted specimen next to the table instantly transports you to the Mediterranean, even if it is a typical summer day.

with colorful cushions. Director's-style folding chairs are great—comfortable, cheap, and easy to fold away at the end of the summer. Deckchairs never seem to date. Outdoor beanbags are fun and super comfortable, come in seductive colors, are water-resistant, and the perfect place to digest the Sunday papers. It takes temptation indeed to coax me from my pink lounger-style beanbag from June to September. You can buy outdoor cushions with plastic backs so they don't get damp—but indoor ones will do just as well, as long as you remember to bring them in before the dew and don't agonize too much if they get ketchup on them.

Tripping the light fantastic?

Who hasn't spent an evening holding their fork over a tea light in the hope of seeing whether any slugs have climbed on with the potato salad? Yes, garden lighting has to be strong enough to let you see what you're eating, but only just. You don't want to feel you're eating in a bus station. Candles, tiki torches (garden flares), and string (fairy) lights are your twinkly friends.

I'm a big believer in more is more in the candle department, which is another way of saying, I'm a tea-light junkie. I buy big bags of them and dot them around the table and all over the garden in jam jars or little lanterns, hanging them from walls, trees, and the arbor. Of course this means that I then spend much of the evening dashing round replacing the things when they burn out, but, I tell myself, it's a small price to pay for ambience. Tiki torches (garden flares) are even easier because they burn happily for hours. Just don't stick them too near your plants or they'll go up in smoke—that herby fragrance you think is the steak marinade might just be your prize bay tree. On the table, I go for a couple of massive white candles placed in hurricane glasses to keep them from blowing out in the slightest breeze.

But the easiest way of all to transform a dingy terrace is good old string (fairy) lights. Wrap them in the branches of trees, around balconies, hang them on an outside wall. You can't really go wrong with these, unless you leave the slack across a doorway and hospitalize your guests. Colored ones have a certain Greek taverna appeal. Kitsch fans might like lights shaped like peppers or made up of fabric flowers. But for most of us, simple white lights are just perfect.

Al Fresco Drinks for Party Time

r A mojito to banish a day at the office

A vacation in Cuba a few years ago left me so unimpressed with the island's cuisine that I left seven pounds lighter (that'll be dry chicken with boiled rice and half a tomato again, then). Still, all wasn't lost—I began a love affair with its famous cocktail. Grow mint yourself and you can always be an arm's length away from some Caribbean escapism. And you won't even have to eat the food.

Makes 1 glass

14 fresh mint leaves, plus a sprig to decorate—garden mint (*Mentha spicata*), otherwise known as spearmint, is best, but any will do
1½ tsp. white sugar (preferably superfine [caster])
juice of ½ a lime
4 large ice cubes
2 measures (2 fl. oz. [50 mL]) light rum
2 splashes of angostura bitters (not essential, but they do add a unique flavor)
sparkling mineral water

Put the mint leaves, sugar, and lime juice in a tumbler glass and mash it all together a bit with a fork or spoon to bring out the mint flavor. Fill the glass with crushed ice (either bash your ice cubes in a pestle and mortar or put them in a tea towel and crush with a rolling pin). Add the rum and angostura bitters, and top with sparkling water and a sprig of mint.

r A fruitful Pimm's

You don't need to be punting down a river to enjoy the definitive English drink of summer, that heady blend of lemonade, gin, bitter herbs, and summer fruit. You don't even have to be English. It's a great way to show off your fresh strawberries, cucumber, mint, and borage flowers. Don't overdo the parts, though; you don't want to feel like you're drinking a meadow.

Serves 6

Pimm's No. 1 cup
1 large bottle of lemonade
1 small homegrown cucumber (or one-third of a store-bought one)
2 handfuls of freshly picked strawberries
freshly picked mint sprigs
about 10 borage flowers
plenty of ice cubes

Mix 1 part Pimm's to 4 parts lemonade in a large jug, leaving one-third of the space at the top to allow for the fruit. Slice the cucumber thinly lengthwise (or across if a larger store-bought one). Halve or quarter the strawberries, depending on how big they are. Add the ice cubes, strawberries, cucumber, and mint, and give it all a quick stir. Finally, add the borage flowers on the top and serve.

Easy Garden-Fresh Hors D'oeuvres

r Quick, easy, and delicious bruschetta

A great way to show off the flavor of just-picked, homegrown tomatoes, and one of my favorite edible garden recipes. It also makes the most of other crops you could be growing such as garlic and basil. Quickly thrown together and irresistibly scrumptious.

Serves 4 as a generous snack
  4 ciabatta rolls
  2 garlic cloves
  extra virgin olive oil
  4 or 5 handfuls of freshly picked tomatoes
  1 handful of freshly picked basil leaves
  sea salt and freshly ground black pepper

Slice the ciabattas in half and toast them lightly. Then rub one side of each with a garlic clove (using the bread almost like a grater). Drizzle a little olive oil. Chop the tomatoes finely (no need to skin them) and heap them on top of the slices, then top with torn basil leaves. Drizzle with more olive oil, and season with salt and pepper.

Serve outside with cold white wine on a hot day.

r The very freshest tzatziki

This is a great impromptu dip to bring out when you have a few friends over. It's also delicious with barbecued meat. It only takes about 15 minutes to make.

Serves 4–6
  3 homegrown cucumbers, picked small
    (about 4 in. [10 cm] long)
  8½ fl. oz. (250 mL) Greek yogurt
  1 generous handful of freshly picked mint,
    stems removed and leaves chopped
  1 garlic clove, crushed
  couple of squeezes of lemon juice, optional

Peel the cucumbers and then halve them lengthwise. Remove the seeds and then grate or finely chop the flesh. Pour the yogurt into a bowl and mix in the other ingredients, including the cucumber.

Serve with raw carrots, breadsticks, mini falafels, or toasted wedges of pita bread or with roast pork or lamb.

What to Do with All These Flowers?

You've gone to the trouble of making a salad. Why not throw a few vividly colored, edible petals on top? They bring a subtle peppery flavor and look irresistible. You don't need many petals—four or five nasturtiums and a couple of heartsease violas or borage flowers, say, is enough.

And for my next trick . . .

If you're drinking white wine, try popping a borage flower into each glass at the table at the last minute. The blue star-shaped flowers turn a beautiful pink when they come into contact with the acid in the wine.

Very nice ice

If, after making your cocktails, your hosting zeal still isn't spent, why not really push the boat out? Freeze edible flowers in ice cubes and add them to cocktails, fruit juices, or just plain water in a jug. Your friends will be floored with admiration as they see perfect orange nasturtiums and viola flowers, suspended in pure ice, floating in their glass. Either that or they'll think something has fallen in from the shrubbery.

The only slightly odd thing about making these exquisite ice cubes is that you have to use distilled water. Otherwise, the ice cube goes all cloudy, which ruins the effect. Buy distilled water from supermarkets and then half fill an ice-cube tray with it and freeze. Pick a few nasturtiums, violas, borage flowers, raspberries, blueberries, sprigs of mint, or anything else in the garden you think will look nice and lay them on the ice, then fill to the top with more distilled water and freeze. And there you go, decorative ice cubes to make any drink a work of art. Bree Van de Kamp would be proud of you.

Autumn

AUTUMN IS AN INDECISIVE BEAST. It can feel damp and spiderweb draped one day and as hot and dry as midsummer the next. At the beginning of the season, you think summer will never end, with sweet corn, runner beans, tomatoes, zucchini (courgettes), figs, raspberries, chard, eggplants (aubergines), blackberries, salad, and peppers reaching lush ripeness. But as the season marches on, there's a chill in the evening air.

Even with crops in containers on a small balcony you'll begin to notice the change. While some, such as zucchini, runner beans, and tomatoes, keep going for a month yet, others are starting to look a little tired, with leaves starting to yellow. But don't put away your garden trowel just yet. If you want fresh salads over winter and succulent fava (broad) beans next spring, this is the time to sow them while there's still warmth in the soil.

Sow much to do . . .

It's also time to plant blackberries and raspberries for lush crops next year. And why not pop in some garlic and order some small plants of chard, either from garden centers or over the internet? With their vivid red, pink, and orange stems, as lurid as highlighter pens, 'Bright Lights' chard shines as bright as a beacon in pots or borders as autumn moves on into winter.

All manner of wonderful salad crops can be sown or planted now—from winter lettuces to the watercress-like land cress, succulent winter purslane, mâche (lamb's lettuce), and exotic-sounding oriental greens such as mizuna, mibuna, and komatsuna, so good eaten raw, lightly steamed, or added to stir-fries. Sown now or bought as ready-grown plants, you can be looking forward to virus-busting salads over the winter months.

And don't forget the flowers. Spring wouldn't be the same without tulips, and even a couple of pots on a balcony look glorious. Why not plant pure white or crimson red tulip bulbs in the same pots as salad—they look great standing sentry above a sea of frilly leaves. Alliums are another showstopper, especially the enormous *Christophii*, a ball of purple stars on a tall stem. Plant now in pots or garden beds for fireworks next summer.

If you do only three things this season:

SOW	PLANT	SOW

fava (broad) beans	garlic	winter salad leaves

Winter Salad Leaves

Mibuna

Growing winter salad leaves is great because you can indulge wildly in cakes, mince pies, chocolate, and cheese over the Christmas period in the knowledge that tomorrow, when you feel utterly sick of carbs, you can pick a crisp, homegrown side salad and feel virtuous about yourself again. A salad dressed with a sweet honey and balsamic dressing to counteract the piquancy of some of these winter leaves is a wonderfully refreshing thing, and is particularly good when topped with some shavings of Parmesan or crumbles of creamy blue cheese.

There are all sorts of delicious salad leaves you can sow in early autumn that will be ready to crop all through the winter and into next spring. It does have to be early autumn, mind you, when there's still warmth in the sun and soil and time for the plants to get to a decent size before winter stops them in their tracks.

These plants are all hardy—that is, they will survive frosts—though it's best to sow them in the warmest, most sheltered spots of your garden or to cover them with floating row cover (garden fabric) to get the best out of them. If you're growing them in a container, place it in a sheltered spot. A window box of feathery green leaves is rather refreshing to look out on.

Unless stated otherwise, thinly sow seeds directly into garden soil or a container filled with potting mix and barely cover with mix or soil. To harvest, either snip off individual leaves and add to salads—in which case the plant will resprout once or twice—or pull up whole plants.

Winter purslane

A plant of many names—*Claytonia perfoliata* and miner's lettuce among them—this is a very pretty salad crop, with scallop-shaped, succulent leaves and stems with a refreshing, citrusy crunch. The leaves also have white flowers in the center, like tiny jewels. The seeds are tiny, so don't do what I did first time and pour them all out on one spot by mistake. Mixing the seeds with a little sand helps to sow them farther apart.

Winter purslane has a handy habit of seeding itself. Once sown and left to flower, it will pop up all over the place come spring next year. Don't weed these seedlings, leave them, and you'll have another crop of winter purslane to enjoy next autumn and winter.

Winter purslane

Mâche (lamb's lettuce)

Arugula (rocket)

Mizuna

Mizuna

Feathery leaves rather like spikier, more robust arugula (rocket) works well as an edging for borders. Its flavor is also similar to arugula, though less spicy.

Mibuna

Strap-like, narrow leaves and a similar taste to mizuna. Works well as a border.

Mâche (lamb's lettuce)

Otherwise known as lamb's lettuce or corn salad, mâche is an exceptionally hardy, low-growing, rosette-forming plant with a lovely mild flavor that counterbalances the pepperiness of many other salad leaves available at this time of year. No wonder it's a staple of store-bought salad bags. It is, however, slow-growing, so don't expect to be eating it until spring.

Arugula (rocket)

Not quite as hardy as the oriental leaves mizuna and mibuna, but worth trying an early autumn sowing.

Early yellow-rocket (land cress: *Barbarea verna*)

Exceptionally hardy salad plant with a taste almost identical to watercress. Serrated, low-growing leaves. Peppery, so use sparingly in salads.

Komatsuna

Tasting like a mix between cabbage and mustard, with a hint of spinach, this is a super-hardy, very useful salad leaf, which is also good in stir-fries.

Buckler-leaf sorrel (French sorrel)

Delicious, tangy lemon taste and small, tender leaves shaped like little shields. Ideal for adding to salads or, if left to mature, it makes a delicious soup.

Chervil

Herb with a delicate aniseedy taste and feathery leaves, delicious chopped and added to steamed carrots or fava (broad) beans. Sow in early autumn and you'll have these hardy leaves all winter.

Komatsuna

Buckler-leaf sorrel
(French sorrel)

Chervil

Fava (Broad) Beans

Hannibal Lecter has a lot to answer for. As if the "fa-fa-fa-fava bean" didn't have enough of an image problem before he weighed in with his unusual cooking advice. The fava beans of my childhood were as appetizing as a plate of leathery, gray saddlebags, but grow them yourself and a whole new world of fava bean opens up. Eat them small and sweet and they're absolutely delicious, full of the flavor of spring and with a bright green vibrancy.

Hardy, hefty creatures, fava beans laugh in the face of frost and snow. Everything about them is reassuringly tough, from the enormous seeds that can be sown directly into garden soil to the pointy,

gray-green leaves and clusters of pods that start to swell in mid-spring. They're a welcome splash of green over the winter months, and plants produce their first delicious baby beans in late spring, when pickings from the garden are otherwise slim. I have been known to get so excited about this first new crop of the year that I pick them far too small and then lose them down the kitchen drain. Hopefully, you'll have more self-control.

The taller varieties have a tendency to flop about like the aftermath of a bachelor weekend, so tie them in to a teepee or prop up with twiggy sticks. Alternatively, go for a dwarf variety such as 'The Sutton' that won't need any support—this is the one to choose for pots. If you want something different, the Crimson-flowered bean is beautiful, an heirloom form with striking red flowers. Just make sure any seeds you sow at this point in the year are suitable for autumn sowing.

Sowing fava beans

When? Mid- to late autumn (you can also sow some varieties in spring, but I always think there's already enough to do at that time of year)

In Pots

container at least 10 in. (25 cm) in diameter with drainage holes • all-purpose potting mix • dwarf fava bean seeds • 30 minutes

How? Add a layer of crocks to the bottom of the container and fill almost to the top with potting mix. Push in the seeds 2 in. (5 cm) deep and about 4 in. (10 cm) apart (or about five seeds to a 10 in. [25 cm] pot). Water and place in a sunny, sheltered spot.

In Soil

stakes or an obelisk • fava bean seeds • 30 minutes

How? If using an obelisk, push it into the ground in a sunny, sheltered spot with well-cultivated soil. Sow about six seeds around the base of the obelisk 2 in. (5 cm) deep. Water well. If using stakes as support, sow seeds 4 in. (10 cm) apart, then push the stakes in among them.

What next? Green shoots should appear within 2–3 weeks, after which they'll need no real attention over the winter unless they're in pots, in which case you may need to water occasionally to stop them from drying out.

What have I done wrong? Fava beans are tough brutes, but in the spring their tips do have a nasty habit of becoming infested with black bean aphids.

t Beans in spring

Fava (broad) beans that were sown in the autumn should be going great guns by mid-spring. Once the first pods have formed, pinch out the tips of the plants with your fingers. It keeps the plants from getting black bean aphids and the shoots are delicious steamed, tasting like a cross between beans and spinach.

Garlic

When I was young I had a posh friend whose mother would waft around the garden in a floppy hat carrying a basket. I was deeply intimidated by her and her Brideshead vowels, but loved her kitchen, the ceiling of which was hung with dried herbs, onions, and garlic, all gathered from her beautiful, walled kitchen garden. The whole room would be filled with the fragrance of drying rosemary and thyme, but it was the garlic, braided and plump, that fascinated me most. It seemed so glamorous and foreign—the image of a more exotic climate.

I still think there's something wondrous about garlic, the way you pop one clove into the ground and it miraculously splits into a whole head of the stuff a few months later. But it couldn't be easier to grow, even in a northern climate. Garlic must be a contender for the lowest-maintenance vegetable award. My own small urban garden keeps us self-sufficient in the stuff, and I still find something romantic about a bunch of my own dried garlic, dried earth still clinging to the roots, hanging from the cupboard door. Sometimes it even kids me into thinking I'm a good cook. There's a real pleasure in the ritual of prying out a clove, unwrapping the papery skin, and chopping a bulb as the beginning to pretty much every dish—from pasta sauces to casseroles and soups.

Choose "wet" or hardneck garlic such as 'Early Wight' or 'Purple Wight.' These don't keep for long but are ready by late spring and have a delicious mild, fresh flavor. Or go for the more common softneck kinds such as 'Solent Wight' that store for months, and the Elephant garlic (really a type of leek) with massive bulbs with a mild flavor. 'Albigensian Wight' from southwest France is a white-skinned bumpy one that keeps for ages.

Planting garlic
When? Mid-autumn to early winter

In Pots

container at least 18 in. (45 cm) in diameter with drainage holes • all-purpose potting mix • garlic cloves • 20 minutes

How? Add a layer of crocks to the container and fill almost to the top with potting mix. Break the head of garlic up into cloves and push them into the potting mix flat end down so the pointy bit is just below the surface. Water and place in a sunny spot.

In Soil

garlic cloves • 15 minutes

How? Choose a sunny spot with well-cultivated soil. Garlic is happy in pretty much any soil, but does like good drainage, so if you have a heavy clay, add compost to the planting hole first. Plant as for pots, above.

What next? Over the next few weeks, you'll see the spiky green shoots come up—they'll provide welcome green over the winter and require nothing more from you until spring when they'll benefit from the odd watering. Dig up the garlic in the summer (or spring for very early varieties) after planting when the leaves start to yellow.

Where have I gone wrong? Garlic is rarely troubled by pests and diseases though occasionally it suffers from white rot or rust.

t Can't I just plant garlic from the supermarket?

Well, you could, but chances are it's been imported so won't be a variety that grows well in your climate. Better to buy from a garden center or check out a specialty supplier—you'll also get a much wider choice of varieties that way.

Autumn Jobs

Bring in the heat lovers

When? Mid-autumn

As autumn gets into its stride, the days may still be warm and sunny, but the nights turn chilly. It's around this time that it's a good idea to bring the hot-blooded plants in pots in your garden inside to a sunny windowsill or room so that their fruits can ripen. Peppers, eggplants (aubergines), and tomatoes will all benefit from this move to warmer climes.

It's also a good time to bring in your tender herbs to a sunny windowsill. Basil, mint, tarragon, and chives can keep going right through winter if you do this. Bring in basil and tarragon plants in their pots. If your mint is planted in the soil, first cut back the dead, twiggy stems right down to ground level, then, using a hand trowel, dig up a patch of roots big enough for a medium-sized pot. Add potting mix to the bottom of the pot, then put the mint roots in and firm in, adding more potting mix if necessary. Water well. Within a week you'll see new green shoots coming up—perfect for making an impromptu mint sauce.

Give green tomatoes a banana-powered nudge

When? Mid-autumn

If your tomatoes are in pots that are too big to move and the fruits are still green by mid-autumn, they're unlikely to ripen this year. Cut the tomatoes off and place in a paper bag with a ripe banana. This gives off a plant-ripening hormone called *ethylene*, which helps ripen the tomatoes.

Figs: you've got to be cruel to be kind

When? Mid-autumn

Look, I know you won't want to hear this, but by mid-autumn, any figs that haven't already ripened won't. All they'll do is hang around, wasting the tree's energy, and then drop off. You've got to move on. Remove any figs that are cherry sized or bigger. Any that are smaller than this are the new figs that will develop next year so leave these. By late autumn/early winter, whenever the first frosts are drawing near, cover your tree with a frost blanket to protect these embryo fruits from the cold. This gives them the very best chance of growing into nice succulent fruits by next summer.

Sow microgreens for winter

- Amaranth
- Basil
- Beets (beetroot)
- Chervil
- Sorrel
- Celery
- Kale
- Mustards like mizuna and mibuna
- Cilantro (coriander)
- Peas
- Sunflowers—harvest after the first pair of leaves emerges or they can turn bitter

When it's too cold to grow outside, why not move indoors? Microgreens are crops sown and harvested when they are only a few days older than a shoot. As long as you have a sunny indoor windowsill, you can sow, grow, and harvest these delicious little bursts of flavor all in the space of about three weeks.

Simply sow the seeds thickly in shallow seed trays of all-purpose potting mix and keep moist. Harvest when the second pair of leaves has grown.

Get distracted online

Why be tied down to watering vulnerable seedlings you've sown yourself when you could let someone else do all the hard work for you? Most plant companies these days send out plants by mail. Shopping this way is surprisingly addictive. I've spent many happy half-hours online browsing through photos of perfect chard and frilly lettuces when I should be working. Why not order some winter salad plants and chard now? Most even have "winter collections" so you don't even need to choose specific plants.

Once you've ordered, they'll email you to tell you when they've been shipped so you can arrange to be in. It's always worth asking the company to leave the package with a neighbor if you're out to save having to wait in post office lines. Hopefully your neighbor can read the instruction "Live Plants" written on the side of the box and won't leave it under the stairs for two weeks before telling you.

r Speedy squash

For a gorgeous, super-fast lunch, take a squash (such as a butternut, 'Uchiki Kuri,' or 'Blue Hubbard'), cut it in half, and scoop out the seeds. Then put a hunk of butter in the middle, put the halves back together, and pop in the microwave on high for about six minutes (checking it now and then to make sure it doesn't overcook). Season with salt and pepper, and scoop straight out of the skin with a spoon.

And to those sowing snobs who say, "But aren't they expensive?" I'd say, "What's better? Sowing loads of seedlings, spending lots of time watering them, and then watching lots of them die because you went away for the weekend, or getting a handful of impeccably healthy plants through the door and planting them all in five minutes?"

Harvesting squashes and pumpkins

Your squashes and pumpkin vines should be trailing all over the place by autumn and have produced several decent-sized fruits. Leave them on the vines until mid-autumn but before the first frosts. Then cut them off. You could either then eat them straightaway or, if you want to store them, leave them out in the sun for a few days to "cure" (or bring them inside to a sunny windowsill if you have room). This makes the skin nice and hard so preserves them longer. You can then keep them over winter or cut little eyes and a mouth out of them for Halloween.

p Greens for wok and health

This box of bountiful leafiness will keep you in refreshing, vitamin-packed salads and stir-fries however dark and short the winter days. Sown in early autumn, it will keep growing throughout the winter months and into the spring. Keep snipping off the leaves a couple of inches from soil level, and each plant should produce two or three times more.

You will need
  1 large window box with drainage holes
  all-purpose potting mix
  1 packet of oriental salad mix seeds
  1 packet of winter purslane (*Claytonia perfoliata*) seeds
  30 minutes

Add a layer of crocks to the bottom of the box, and then fill it almost to the top with potting mix. Sprinkle your oriental salad mix thinly over the surface, leaving some space at each end. In this space, sprinkle the winter purslane seeds (beware, these are really tiny so this is best done a pinch at a time) as thinly as you can and then barely cover all with more potting mix and water.

Within ten days or so small shoots will begin to emerge. Oriental salad mixes usually contain a combination of mizuna, the feathery green salad leaf a little like arugula (rocket) though less spicy, mibuna (a non-feathery version), pak choi, red mustard, komatsuna, and Chinese cabbage. Either snip the leaves off young, leaving a few inches above soil level so the plant can regrow, or wait until the leaves are a bit bigger and use them in a stir-fry.

A salad of these leaves with strips of bacon and a creamy salad dressing to offset the pepperiness of some of the leaves is truly heavenly. The addition of the succulent, slightly lemony winter purslane gives the whole mix a welcome crunch.

Winter Lettuce

It's nice having a nice selection of well-flavored, variously textured salad leaves, but they can seem a little insubstantial on their own. To make a really good winter salad you need some crunch and substance, too, and this is where winter lettuces come in.

I always sow a few in early autumn in seed trays to transplant when they are big enough. One of my favorites is 'Winter Density,' a romaine type with sweet, crunchy stems. Other good winter varieties include 'Black Seeded Simpson,' which has wrinkled leaves, 'Reine de Glace,' with its robust yet mild-flavored leaves, the sword-shaped 'Cocarde,' the traditional soft, round 'Valdor,' and the beautifully colored and very hardy 'Red Sails.'

All these lettuces are hardy and should survive outdoors all winter, but it has to be said that you'll get more tender leaves and faster growth if you put some floating row cover (garden fabric) over them. I find the tunnels very cool—ready-made hoops with fleece attached that you can just concertina out into a tunnel and pop over a couple of decent rows. For plants in pots, you could wrap them in a frost blanket instead.

Cloche to protect lettuces.

Sowing winter lettuces

When? Early autumn

Where? In seed starting trays inside on a windowsill or outside in a sheltered spot.

How? Fill the seed starting tray cells with potting mix and then tap the tray down gently to settle the potting mix and water so the surface of the potting mix is damp. Leave to drain for a couple of minutes, then place two seeds on the surface of the potting mix in each cell and barely cover with potting mix.

What next? When the seedlings have germinated and are about ½ in. (1 cm) high (a couple of weeks), pinch off the weaker seedlings at soil level. Keep the potting mix moist and when the seedlings have six true leaves, plant out into your garden soil about 8 in. (20 cm) apart. If growing in a pot, you can fit about five in a 12 in. (30 cm) diameter pot. To harvest, either snip off individual leaves from the outside or leave the lettuces to heart up and cut the whole plant off at the base when mature.

Blackberries

Why would you bother growing something that can rip your hands to pieces and that you can get for free from the grassy edges of most country roads? It's a sensible question. So resistant have I always been to the thought of growing a cultivated strain of blackberry that it was only last year that one finally crept into my garden. But I'm now a total convert. First, they're one of the few edible crops that are happy growing up a shady wall—and how many urban gardeners among us have one of those? Second, you can buy thornless kinds that won't lacerate your fingers. Third, they can be trained in loop-the-loop shapes down the wall or fence, which looks really cool, even in winter. And fourth, the taste and size of some of these cultivated varieties puts their wild cousins to shame.

For ease of picking, choose a thornless variety such as 'Waldo' or 'Oregon Thornless,' which has the added bonus of a fairly compact habit and pretty, dark green, parsley-like leaves.

Planting blackberries

When? Any time, though autumn gives the plant's roots plenty of time to establish before the growing season starts in spring

Where? Choose a sunny or shady spot near a fence with well-cultivated soil that has preferably had compost or well-rotted manure added

How? Dig a hole big enough for the plant. Take it out of the pot and plant it in the hole. Attach screw eyes (vine eyes)—basically a ring on the end of a screw that you can attach to the fence or wall and thread wire through (if it's a fence you can simply screw them in by hand, though you may want to make guide holes with a drill first; if it's a wall you may need to drill a hole and insert a screw anchor first). Then thread wire through them so that you end up with three parallel wires at roughly equal distance from each other up the fence.

What next? Keep the plant watered. Tie in new canes to the wires as they develop, looping them up and down like a rollercoaster to fit in the longest shoots possible in the space you have. Blackberries grow in a fairly unusual way. In the first year, one or more long, loopy shoots will grow. Tie these in. In the second year, these shoots will bear fruit while the plant also puts out new shoots from the base that need tying in. To avoid getting all of these shoots into an unholy muddle, it's best to keep the old and new shoots separate, tying them in to different sides of the plant. The result is an attractive and unusual-shaped plant.

Where have I gone wrong? Raspberry beetle is an occasional pest.

Raspberries

If raspberry bushes were people, they'd be dependable sorts who would always turn up on time and never forget your birthday. They just get on with it, needing very little attention, but churning out their velvety berries for months, filling bowl after bowl. I planted three bushes (known as canes) in my garden two years ago and this year must have had enough raspberries to open a small farm stand.

For this reason alone—and, of course, the lush, juicy taste, but that goes without saying—raspberries are a good bet for a small edible garden owned by a busy person. They do need to be planted in the ground, though, since their naturally spreading habit makes them unhappy in containers.

Unfortunately, the traditional way of growing raspberries seems to require an engineering degree and a very large tool kit. I'm talking of the dizzyingly sturdy post and wire support system that the books bang on about. I've tried this and the result was a bleak winter's evening with a power drill and a large stake, diminishing light and, eventually, tears. I'm not saying you're as rubbish as I am at DIY, but please. All you want to do is grow some berries, not construct an aerial assault course for paratroopers.

This is why I only grow 'Autumn Bliss' since, like all autumn-fruiting varieties, it needs no support and takes up less room. It's also dripping with berries in autumn when so much in the garden is beginning to wind up for the year. Other good autumn-fruiting varieties are 'Joan J' and the golden 'Fallgold.' You can buy 'Autumn Bliss' canes in pots in spring, but the usual time to plant them is as 'bare-rooted canes' in late autumn or winter. When these arrive, don't panic. They will look like something you'd throw to your dog in the park, but are actually alive.

And if you're worried that by planting only an autumn-fruiting variety you're missing out on summer berries, think again . . . with a simple, nifty pruning tip, you can have raspberries from June to October (see page 147).

Planting raspberries

When? Late autumn/winter

Where? Choose a sunny or partially shaded spot with well-cultivated soil that has preferably had lots of compost or well-rotted manure added to it.

How? Dig a hole big enough for the roots of the cane to spread out without cramping. Cover with soil, making sure that the soil level is the same as it was at the nursery (you should see a line on the cane where the soil came to). Repeat, spacing your canes about 20 in. (50 cm) apart. With pruners, now cut each cane back to about 8 in. (20 cm) above the ground.

What next? Nothing until harvest time next year.

Where have I gone wrong? Raspberries don't get bothered by pests and diseases much, but might be attacked by aphids or raspberry beetle.

r Crisp raspberry and cream stacks

Tossing raspberries straight into my mouth in the garden is usually as far as I get when it comes to making fancy fruit puddings. But this one occasionally tempts me into the kitchen. It looks like more of a big deal than it actually is so could make someone special think you're amazing. It can also be made with strawberries.

Serves 2

ready-made phyllo pastry, enough for 8 rectangles about 4 in. (10 cm) by 2 in. (5 cm)

7 fl. oz. (200 mL) heavy whipping (double) cream

9 oz. (250 g) raspberries

confectioners' (icing) sugar, for sprinkling

2 mint sprigs

Cut the pastry into rectangles using a sharp knife. Don't worry if they're not exactly the same size, we're not aiming for perfection. Lay them on parchment paper on a baking sheet and bake in a hot oven for 3–4 minutes or until they are crisp. Meanwhile, whip the cream.

When the pastry is cool, brush off any excess flour and layer them with the cream and raspberries between them, adding a generous sprinkle of icing sugar to each layer, making two stacks. Sprinkle more confectioners' sugar on the top and pop a mint sprig on each if you're feeling particularly fancy. Serve immediately while the pastry is at its crispiest.

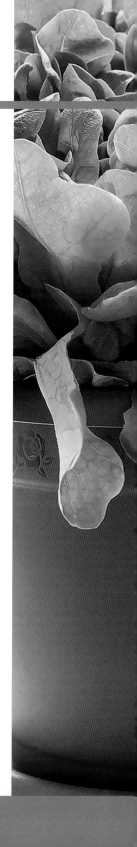

Winter

I T'S THE SEASON OF CHRISTMAS, radiators on full-blast, joining a gym and then going only once. It's a time to ignore the garden, isn't it? Well, you can if you want, but nature has a comforting way of never quite stopping the clock. It may not be the time for sowing anything much right now, but there are still things you could be picking—kale and chard for fireside roast lunches, mizuna and mibuna for stir-fries, and chicory (endive), mâche (corn salad), winter purslane, arugula (rocket), and winter lettuce for salads so detoxifying and virtuous you can follow them with sticky toffee pudding and not hate yourself. And the benefit of growing it all outside your back door is you only have to pop out into the cold for a moment to get it.

If you do only three things this season:

PLANT

a couple of fruit trees

BUY

seeds

ORDER

potatoes

Beat the Cold, Plant a Tree

For the energetic, winter is the time to plant fruit trees. Even a tiny balcony has room for a couple of apples, a cherry, or a plum. Or why not go a bit exotic with an apricot or peach? Fruit trees in pots are much easier to grow than you might think. As for me, as the winter weather bites, I'm usually to be found online, clicking through pictures of exotic peppers, weird-looking squashes, and blue potatoes, and dreaming about how amazing my garden is going to be next year. Again. Ordering seeds with your feet jammed into slippers shaped like rabbits might not be glamorous, but it beats moping on the sofa in front of the television.

Don't think you need vast acres and a team of gardeners to produce delicious fruit from your garden. My little urban patch houses two pears, a plum, a fan-trained peach and apricot, and two apple trees all in a space so small you could barely swing a chandelier. They're easier to grow than you might think.

In pots

Short, skinny fruit trees are great for people with small gardens. They grow upright in a column shape with very short branches so you can plant them in pots and fit them into a small space like a terrace or balcony. You can get apples, pears, cherries, and plums grown this way. Why not get all four and have your own mini orchard?

The bare-root of the matter

Look, I know winter is probably the time you least feel like going outside and planting a fruit tree. It's cold, it's dirty and, anyway, the tree you ordered looks like a twig. But bear with me.

You can buy fruit trees all year round. A garden center in midsummer will have pretty much any type of fruit tree for sale, all grown in pots. These are fine, but are sometimes dehydrated and pot-bound. You also won't get anywhere near the variety you would get from a specialty supplier. Order a bare-root tree online over the winter months and you don't even have to lug anything into the back of the car. You'll get a far greater variety to choose

from, and they'll be much cheaper and probably healthier, too.

A "bare-root tree" is called that because it arrives looking like a tree that's been pulled out of the ground by a giant. Its roots dangle in midair and the branches look like something you'd put on the fire. But it's not dead, it's sleeping and, come spring, its leaves will unfurl. I did try telling that to a train-full of passengers when I took an apricot tree across London last winter, but they still looked at me like I'd escaped from a secure unit.

Against walls and fences

If you have a garden, why not try a beautiful ready-trained fruit tree? They come in some attractive shapes and look nice even in winter. Climbers, shaped like acute accents, handsome multitiered espaliers, single-Us, fans . . . there are all sorts of forms available that will love a warm wall or fence. They take years to get into these shapes and take some skill so buy them ready-trained unless you're a total masochist.

Apples and Pears

They may not be exotic, but guess what, that means you're more likely to get a decent harvest. Good pear varieties include 'Concorde,' 'Buerré Hardy,' or 'Doyenné du Comice'. As for apples, there are so many varieties to choose from it's almost dizzying, but 'Discovery,' 'Braeburn,' 'Cox,' and 'James Grieve' are all gorgeous. You might have to buy more than one tree for the best pollination—check with the suppliers. Best varieties for growing in pots include 'Sunset,' 'Scrumptious,' 'Red Windsor,' or 'Red Falstaff.' Choose a tree grown on an M27 rootstock so it won't grow taller than about 3 ft. (1 m) and plant it in a large pot that can take 1½–2 cu. ft. (40–60 L) of potting mix. As for the potting mix go for a soil-based mix that contains more nutrients for these long-term crops.

Pears need an even bigger pot—one that takes about 3½ cu. ft. (100 L) of potting mix and make sure it's on Quince Eline rootstock. Best pear varieties for pots are 'Beth,' 'Concorde,' 'William,' and 'Louise Bonne of Jersey.'

r Cinnamon apple crisps

The best way to enjoy the harvest of a young apple tree is fresh off the branch. But when your tree gets more mature it might produce more apples than you can eat at harvest time, which is where this nifty recipe comes in. You don't need any special equipment to make these delicious, crunchy crisps, and they keep in a jar or can (tin) for weeks (though they're so delectable (moreish) chances are you'll eat them all in a day).

Serves 2
2 sweet apples
½ tsp. cinnamon
1½ tsp. granulated sugar

Heat the oven to 230°F (110°C). Core the apples and then slice them across the middle to make thin rings about 1 mm thick (no need to peel them). If you have a mandoline this would be a good time to use it, but a knife will do. Lay them in a single layer on a baking tray on parchment paper. Mix the sugar and cinnamon together then sprinkle it over the apples. Bake for around 45 minutes (but check to make sure they're not burning) turning them halfway through and sprinkling the other side with cinnamon sugar. When the crisps have dried out and are light golden brown, they're ready.

Plums and Cherries

There's something so seductive about plums. They're no-nonsense trees yet their fruits are full-fleshed sensuality itself. Eat them straight off the tree when they're still warm from the sun. Cherries are a great addition to a patio, too. 'Stella' and 'Sunburst' are good cherries, while, for plums, you really can't go wrong with the luscious 'Victoria,' but plant it in the ground since plums don't like growing in containers. You may have to chase the birds off, though—or protect with frost blankets when the fruits are at their ripest and most tempting.

Aim for a large container that holds 3½ cu. ft. (100 L) of potting mix and make sure your tree is on Gisella 5 dwarfing rootstock.

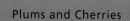

Peaches and Apricots

Eating a sun-warmed, melting-fleshed, homegrown peach or apricot straight off the tree is perhaps the most fun you can have in the garden while sober. Bought peaches and apricots either seem to be as hard as billiard balls or with a texture and taste like cotton wool. But grow them yourself and they're in another league. I'm obsessed with my fan-trained 'Peregrine' peach and fuss around it like a window-dresser in a high-end department store. Buy a ready-trained fan and plant it in the soil or a pot against a sheltered, sunny fence or wall, training the branches into parallel wires. Alternatively, buy a dwarf tree and pop it in a pot in a sunny spot on your terrace.

There is, however, a big black mark against these luscious trees. From autumn to late winter you have to protect them with plastic to prevent peach leaf curl disease (see page 150), which can devastate crops. If in a pot, tuck the tree up under the eaves of the house to protect it from rain. Those in open ground grown against a fence would benefit from being covered with plastic. This can make your garden look like the storeroom of a dry cleaner's. So delicious are the peaches, however, that I'm prepared to make this little sacrifice and, anyway, new resistant varieties are being bred all the time.

Go for white-fleshed 'Peregrine,' the very reliable 'Rochester,' and doughnut-shaped 'Saturn' with its honey-like taste. 'Bonanza' is particularly good in containers. As for apricots, you could do much worse than 'Moorpark,' 'Aprigold,' 'Safon,' or 'Tomcot,' which is particularly reliable in colder locations.

Do Looks Matter?

Winter is a great time to sit down with paper and pencil and seed catalogs and lay out next spring's garden. Feel free to pencil in plants willy-nilly; any plant that's healthy is going to look fairly appealing, wherever you put it. But sometimes it's fun to try and get a bit artistic. The only danger is that, once you start, you become obsessed and refuse to pick that red lettuce because it'll ruin the symmetry of your red-and-green-salad checkerboard bed. If this happens, I'm afraid I can't help you, you're a lost cause.

Mix heights for visual interest

Vary the heights when you're planning a bed. Some plants are so big they act as centerpieces all on their own, such as artichokes and feathery bronze fennel, which can rear up to almost 6½ ft. (2 m). Or grow runner beans, sweet peas, or trailing nasturtiums, cucumbers, or squashes up teepees. Ready-made arches and arbors (pergolas) are worth thinking about too.

Climbing wonders

Artfully clothe your fences or walls not only with blackberries, flowering climbers, or trained fruit trees, such as espalier apples or fan-trained plums, cherries, and peaches, but also with tomatoes, growing up strings tied to the top of the fence. Runner and climbing beans and squashes will also scramble up trellises, as will sweet peas, cucumbers, and climbing zucchini (courgettes).

Design with vegetables

Just like flowers, the colors and textures of vegetables and fruit plants vary wildly and you can create some really dramatic combinations. Try bright and unusually colored varieties—purple green (French) beans, 'Tromboncino' squashes, black tomatoes, yellow snow peas (mangetout), or purple artichokes. Contrast feathery patches of carrots with glossy, large-leaved chard. Make the most of striking structural plants, such as the delicate plume of feathery fennel, whether the green or bronze sort, and contrast with big, bold brassicas or lush-leaved eggplants (aubergines). Salad leaves look particularly varied—from purple to green, frilly to pointed. Plant them in wavy lines, crosses, triangles, squares, checkerboards. . . . Who knew you could express yourself so much with lettuce?

r A decadent winter salad

The slightly peppery winter salad leaves are a wonderful foil here for the lush creaminess of the blue cheese and sweetness of the dressing.

Serves 4 as a starter, 2 as a main
For the salad
3 good handfuls of winter salad leaves (lettuce, arugula [rocket], mizuna, chard . . . whatever you have growing out there), the larger leaves torn into pieces
1 head of endive (chicory), roughly sliced
3½ oz. (100 g) Stilton cheese (or any creamy blue cheese)
1 and a half handfuls of pine nuts
For the dressing
1 Tbsp. cranberry sauce (from a jar)
½ Tbsp. red wine vinegar
½ Tbsp. balsamic vinegar
1 Tbsp. olive oil

Wash the salad leaves thoroughly and put in a large bowl. Add the chicory (endive) and then crumble the cheese on top. Put the pine nuts in a heavy-bottomed pan over a low heat for 3–4 minutes until they turn brown and are toasted, then sprinkle those on the top of the salad.

Put the cranberry sauce, vinegars, and oil into a jar and give it all a good shake. Spoon it on top of the salad and toss well.

Flowers for color

If things start looking boring, add a flower, that's my motto. My garden is roughly two-thirds fruit and vegetables, one-third flowers, and it's a ratio that seems to work. In the height of summer when the cosmos, alliums, and nicotiana are waving high and the nasturtiums a sea of orange, you might not think there were any edible crops in there at all. Flowers bring in pollinating bees and butterflies as well as aphid-munching ones like hoverflies so their appeal may have a practical element too.

Edging

An edging of curly parsley, thyme, chives, spiky arugula (rocket), oriental greens, or strawberries can look rather stylish. Choose plants that are low-growing (so you can see over them to the bed behind) and non-spreading so they keep their neat pattern.

Winter Jobs

Pruning blackberries

When? Early winter

By winter, your blackberry bush will have finished fruiting. Using pruners, cut down all the canes that had fruit on them this year. You will be left with a lopsided bush, with all its canes trained over to one side. When the new canes start to develop in spring, simply tie them in to the other side to balance out the bush again.

Put fruit trees to bed

When? Midwinter

Whenever a plant needs protecting against the cold—a lemon, peach, or fig tree for example—you'll be advised to cover it with "row cover" or "frost blanket." It's a gauzy, thin drape the consistency of a net curtain. How can this provide any protection against the biting cold of a winter's night? Well, it traps a thin layer of warmer air around the plant and this is, in most cases, enough to protect the vulnerable buds or shoots from damage. Or something along those lines . . . I just know it works. I wrap my fig and lemon tree in frost blankets over winter. They have a drawstring and are really pretty cute.

Harvesting radicchio

When? Midwinter

Any radicchio you sowed back in the summer should be looking beautiful by now, with deep burgundy, spiky leaves. I have a pot outside the back door and it really lifts the spirits on yet another glum mid-January day. You can either pick individual outer leaves to add to salads (be warned, they're quite bitter) or harvest the whole plant and grill it, which brings out the sweetness. Cut a whole radicchio head into quarters, brush with olive oil, and grill it for a few minutes each side, then top with cheese and grill until the cheese bubbles.

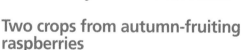

Two crops from autumn-fruiting raspberries

When? Late winter

The usual way to prune autumn-fruiting raspberries is to cut all the canes down to the ground in late winter using pruners. Since I'm a raspberry nut, however, I extend their fruiting season by pruning them slightly differently. In late winter, I cut only half the canes down to the ground. This way, I get raspberries in early summer as well as autumn.

Garden Villains

It's unfortunate, but you won't be the only one wanting to eat the fruit and vegetables you grow. There's a legion of pests out there who fancy their chances, too, and a few diseases that could get in the way of you and edible perfection. We've all been tempted to reach for the slug pellets of doom and the sprays of certain insect annihilation on discovering a fava (broad) bean plant swarming with black bean aphids or a snail trail where treasured carrot seedlings were yesterday, but how do you cope with pests and diseases if you want to garden organically? Armed with vigilance, insecticidal soft soap, and a good squishing finger, you should get the better of the beasts and other ills that can affect your precious specimens. All the disease and pest deterrents listed are organic.

Aphids (greenfly)

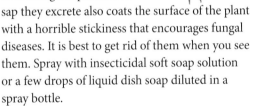

Like black bean aphids, these congregate on the soft growing tips of young plants, sucking the sap and weakening the plants. The sap they excrete also coats the surface of the plant with a horrible stickiness that encourages fungal diseases. It is best to get rid of them when you see them. Spray with insecticidal soft soap solution or a few drops of liquid dish soap diluted in a spray bottle.

Black bean aphids (blackfly)

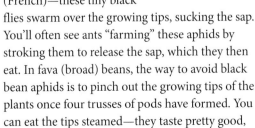

A particular pest of beans—fava (broad), runner, and green (French)—these tiny black flies swarm over the growing tips, sucking the sap. You'll often see ants "farming" these aphids by stroking them to release the sap, which they then eat. In fava (broad) beans, the way to avoid black bean aphids is to pinch out the growing tips of the plants once four trusses of pods have formed. You can eat the tips steamed—they taste pretty good,

like spinach. Otherwise, either blast off the flies with a jet of water or spray with insecticidal soft soap solution, an organic aphid deterrent available from all garden centers. Buy a cheap, plastic spray bottle to apply it with. You could also try diluting a couple of drops of liquid dish soap in a spray bottle and spraying that on for similar results.

Blight

This is a serious fungal disease that affects potatoes and tomatoes. The first signs in potatoes are brown patches on the leaves with white rings around them on the undersides. In tomatoes, similar brown patches appear on the leaves, with blackened patches on the stems. Unfortunately, once the disease has taken hold, there's very little you can do, so it's best to plant blight-resistant varieties. Cut affected potato leaves down to the ground and burn them immediately in the hope that the spores have not yet infected the potato tubers in the ground. With tomatoes, whole crops of fruit can turn black and rotten almost overnight. The disease is worse in damp, cool summers. The good news is that if you only grow early potatoes you are unlikely to be troubled by it.

Blossom end rot

A disease in tomatoes in which a leathery, dark patch appears at the bottom of the fruit. It's caused by irregular watering. Remove any affected fruits and take care to water little and often rather than via an occasional deluge.

Botrytis (gray mold)

Fruits or leaves develop a gray, furry mold that spreads until the whole fruit rots. It's worse during a wet summer. Remove any infected fruit and leaves. When planting lettuces don't bury the leaf bases under the soil.

Carrot rust fly

A serious pest of carrots, these flies lay eggs that hatch into maggots and tunnel into the center of your carrots, causing them to rot. Telltale signs are reddish leaves that wilt in sunny weather. Your only solution to this problem is prevention: the best way is to grow varieties with built-in carrot fly resistance; you can also grow carrots in containers more than 2 ft. (60 cm) above ground level (the flies are lazy fliers); finally, make sure you sow thinly so that you don't have to thin the carrots later, the smell of which can attract the flies.

p How to make your own (safe) insecticide

You will need
quarter of a bar of fragrance-free, dye-free soap
1 qt. (1 L) mineral water
1 Tbsp. vegetable oil
spray bottle
bucket or large bowl
bottle with lid

Drop the soap into the water in the bowl and leave overnight. Remove any soap that has not dissolved. The water should be white. Mix in the vegetable oil, pour into a bottle, and shake well. Spray the solution onto affected leaves and watch the flea beetles run for the hills.

Caterpillars

Large holes in your kale or nasturtium leaves? No slug or snail trails? Look for caterpillars, the most likely culprit. Remove any you see and squash them, and look out for egg clusters on the underside of the leaves and squash these too.

Cats

For cats your best defense is a mat of twiggy branches. See page 57.

Common scab

A disease often seen on potatoes in which scabby, scurfy patches appear on the surface of the tubers. It's only skin deep and doesn't affect the taste so simply scrub off the patches and eat as normal.

Flea beetle

Arugula (rocket) leaves peppered with tiny holes? A cloud of tiny black beetles that fly up when you disturb the leaves? You have flea beetles. A mild infestation doesn't really do your crop any harm, and you won't even notice the little holes in your salad. If you're worried, avoid growing arugula (rocket) between late May and midsummer, since this is the period when these little charmers are most around.

Leaf miner

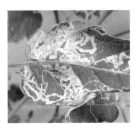

Troublesome maggots that tunnel inside the leaves of beetroot, chard, spinach, and spinach beet creating ugly brown wiggly patches. Once they have eaten part of the leaf, the fully grown larvae then drops down into the soil to overwinter and emerge in spring as an adult fly. The only way to prevent it is to keep an eagle eye on the underside of your leaves and look for small, white eggs. Squash these before they hatch. If you see brown areas on the leaves, squash the maggot inside and remove that part of the leaf before eating.

Peach leaf curl

This is the curse of peaches, apricots, and nectarines, a fungal disease that is spread by rain splash that brings up spores from the ground. For this reason, the recommended prevention is to cover your tree with plastic from autumn to late winter. Admittedly, it's not pretty, but as someone who has lost an entire peach crop to the dreaded plague (lurgy), I'm happy to drape away. Alternatively, if your tree is in a pot, move it under the eaves of your house so it stays out of the rain that way. Signs of the disease are red, puckered leaves in spring, which later fall off.

Powdery mildew

Does it look as though someone has dipped your plant's leaves in talcum powder? Sounds like powdery mildew, a fungal disease caused by bad ventilation, not enough moisture in the soil, and damp air. It's particularly common in peas, zucchinis (courgettes), squashes, and sweet peas and, although unlikely to kill a plant, does weaken it, reduce cropping, and make it look rather grim. Prevent in the first place by not overcrowding your plants. If you have it, try diluting one part milk to nine parts water and spraying the liquid onto the leaves. The proteins in the milk are thought to react somehow with sunlight to produce an antiseptic effect that deals with the mildew spores. Also keep plants well watered and fed, and try to increase ventilation around the plant as much as you can.

Raspberry beetle

A pest of raspberries and blackberries that lays its eggs inside the fruit, making them brown, hard, and inedible. You might find little white grubs in the berries. If you think you've got this pest, immerse the berries in salty water to bring out any unwelcome guests and then rinse them under cold water before eating.

Red spider mite

Usually only seen in indoor plants or outside in particularly hot summers where the dry air encourages these microscopic insects to colonize the leaves and suck the sap. It can be a problem for peppers, cucumbers, and lemon trees. Telltale signs are white web fibers and pale yellow dots on the underside of the leaves. Mist the leaves regularly to keep up humidity. Indoors, a biological control called *Phytoseiulus persimilis* can be effective.

Rust

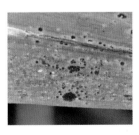

Orange spots on the leaves of garlic. If you see it, harvest your garlic as usual but don't plant it in the same spot for three years.

Scale insect

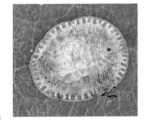

This is a problem for citrus trees. Little shield-like bugs cluster on the undersides of the leaves and in the joints where the leaves meet the stems and suck the sap, weakening the tree. Remove them by hand or with an old toothbrush and soapy water.

Slugs and snails

If you spot them in your garden, gird yourself for battle. See page 56.

Split tomatoes

This is also caused by irregular watering. Take care to water little and often rather than via an occasional deluge.

Whitefly

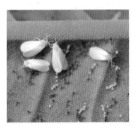

If you see clouds of tiny white moths that fly up from plants when disturbed, chances are you have whitefly. They weaken the plants, and can be a particular problem with young tomato seedlings. Spray with insecticidal soft soap solution or a few drops of liquid dish soap diluted in a spray bottle.

White rot

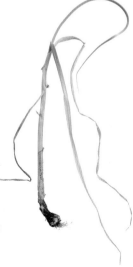

A disease affecting the roots of the allium family—leeks, onions, and garlic—that eventually rots the crop. Telltale signs are fluffy white mold in the soil around the roots and a sickly, yellowing, and wilted plant. Dig up and burn affected plants and don't plant alliums in the same place for at least three years until the disease has left the soil.

Glossary

bolt. A salad plant is said to bolt when it begins to flower. The central stem will begin to shoot upwards to make the flowering stalk. At this point the leaves become too bitter to eat. Bolting is a natural part of the aging process of the plant but can also occur when the plant is stressed through insufficient water so make sure you keep salad crops damp to prevent early bolting.

burn. If you spread manure or compost on the garden that has not rotted down sufficiently, the excess nitrogen in it will dehydrate the plant roots. Plants may take on a yellowish or "burned" appearance. Manure or compost (especially high-nitrogen manures such as from chickens) must be rotted down for at least a year, preferably two or three, before you use them around plants. Put simply, if the manure smells of manure, it is too fresh to use.

cultivar. A variety of plant that has been produced by selective breeding.

cure. To harden the skin of a pumpkin or squash to prevent it from deterioration and develop a sweeter flavor. This is simply done by cutting it from the plant once the stem has hardened and turned brown (leave a couple of inches of stem attached to the fruit). Then take the fruit into a sunny windowsill, carrying it carefully—not by the stem. After two weeks, flip the fruit over to cure the bottom half. Then store them somewhere airy and dry such as a garage, making sure they have air circulation around them by raising them ideally on wire or wooden racks.

deadhead. To remove flowers once they have faded and turned brown. This encourages new flowers to form.

double-digging. A soil preparation method used on extremely compacted soils or those with a clay layer beneath that is stopping water from draining away. Rather than digging to a single spade's depth, which is adequate for other soils, these soils need the clay layer to be broken up, which means digging down do a double depth. Since the top layer of soil is where the vast majority of the organic matter and nutrients is, this soil should be removed and placed aside. The lower level of soil can then be broken up with a fork and gravel or grit added to increase the drainage. The top layer can then be replaced on top.

ericaceous. Suitable for lime-hating plants. An ericaceous (or acidic) potting mix is therefore used when growing blueberries and raspberries, both of which are not happy in limey or alkaline soils.

liquid feed. Useful for pot-grown fruit and vegetables since the potting mix they are growing in (even if new) will run out of nutrients as the plant grows. Liquid seaweed feed is a good organic feed for leafy crops while fruiting crops such as tomatoes benefit from a tomato feed high in potassium to boost their fruit production. If you have space to grow some comfrey plants, they make a great high-potassium feed.

all-purpose potting mix (multipurpose compost). A general use planting medium you buy in plastic sacks from the garden center that is ideal for fruit and vegetables (unless they are acid loving, in

Left: beets (beetroot) harvested from my pots.

which case use **ericaceous**). Generally a mix of rotted garden compost, fertilizer, and bulky organic material, this is a good, light, clean mix for starting seeds off or growing in pots. However, the nutrients in it will be depleted by plants after three weeks after which time you should make sure you feed it with **liquid feed** every couple of weeks. Aim to buy organic and peat-free.

mushroom compost. The compost mushroom farms have left over once they have harvested their crop. It's light, clean, and a great soil conditioner if you can get hold of it. The only thing to remember is that it's slightly alkaline so don't use it on acid-loving crops such as blueberries or raspberries.

organic matter. Sometimes called soil improver or soil conditioner—is any material derived from living matter that is added to the soil to increase nutrients and improve soil composition. Usually farmyard manure or compost is added in spring or autumn.

pinch out. If a plant is becoming too leggy, you are often advised to "pinch out" the growing tip to encourage it to branch at the pinch point and therefore become a bushier plant. In vegetable and fruit growing it is often used to encourage fruit below the pinch point to ripen better. You literally "pinch" with your thumb and third finger since at this stage the shoot is soft enough to remove without pruners (secateurs). In tomato growing we pinch out the side shoots that form between the main stem and leaves to stop them from developing, thereby redirecting the energy of the plant into the fruit that is already ripening.

potash. A potassium compound helpful as a plant fertilizer.

sheltered position. A spot that receives plenty of sunlight and is out of direct winds.

thin out. Since we can't guarantee every seed we sow will germinate, we cover our backs by sowing more than we need. Once they have germinated, we then need to make sure each plant has enough space to develop adequately. This may mean removing some of the seedlings on either side of it. This can be done by hand—carefully trying to avoid damaging the plants next to them. If the plants are big enough to eat, go ahead and do so. It may seem counterintuitive to be removing healthy seedlings, but it is worth it to ensure the remaining ones grow as well as they can.

truss. The tight cluster of fruits growing from one stalk that you see on tomato plants.

tubers. The thickened underground part of a stem. We call the potatoes we plant tubers since this is technically what they are.

variegated. Plants with leaves that contain a second color as well as green. This is usually white or yellow.

Index

al fresco dining and drinks, 114, 118
alliums, 65, 76, 122, 146, 151
amaranth, 131
annual flowers, 63
ants, 148
aphids, 44, 51, 61, 82, 127, 137, 148
apples, 140, 142, 145
apricots, 144–145, 150
artichokes, 92, 145
arugula, 34
arugula (rocket), 94, 125, 133, 146, 150
aubergines. *See* eggplants

barbecues, 113–114, 115
Barefoot breakfast smoothie, 84
basil, 12, 13, 70, 104, 109, 115, 119, 131
baskets, hanging, 18, 56, 76
bay, 72
Beanfest in a box, 82
beans
    fava (broad) (*See* fava (broad) beans)
    green (*See* green (French) beans)
    runner (*See* runner beans)
beets (beetroot), 41, 60, 94, 114, 131, 150
black bean aphids, 82, 127, 148
blackberries, 40, 84, 106, 135, 147
blight, 36, 78, 148–149
blossom end rot, 78, 149
blueberries, 15, 40, 84, 93, 121
borage, 62–63, 120, 121
botrytis (gray mold), 39, 149
breakfast smoothie, 84
bruschetta, 119

Calendula officinalis (marigolds), 63, 82
California poppies, 15, 65
carrot rust fly, 149
carrots, 53, 94, 125, 145
caterpillars, 61, 89, 149
cats, in garden, 56, 149
celery, 131
chamomile, 73
chard, 42–43, 94, 122, 146, 150
cherries, 140, 143, 145
chervil, 71, 115, 125, 131
chicory (endive), 146
Chinese cabbage, 133
chitting, 32, 35, 36
chives, 71, 104, 115, 146
cilantro, 10, 70–71, 108, 109, 115, 131
Cinnamon apple crisps, 142
clematis, 65
climbers, 65, 76, 98–99, 145
comfrey, 97
common scab, 150
compost, 22–24, 26, 28–29, 31, 40
containers, 15–20
coriander. *See* cilantro
corn, sweet, 54, 89, 107
Corn on the cob, 113
corn salad, 125
cosmos, 64, 76, 146
cottage gardens, 99
courgettes. *See* zucchini
Crisp raspberry and cream stacks, 137
cucumbers, 48, 87, 98, 119, 145, 151

dahlias, 65, 76
drainage, 13, 15, 17, 24–25, 92

early yellowrocket, 125
edible flowers, 62–64
eggplants, 10, 51, 88–89, 101, 114, 130
endive (chicory), 146
espaliers, 141

fava (broad) beans, 60, 71, 114–115, 125–127, 148
fennel, 71, 94, 145
fertilizing, 96–97
figs, 15, 40, 66–67, 105, 116, 130
flea beetle, 61, 150
flowering tobacco, 65
flowers, 62–64, 120–121, 146
Frozen herb cubes, 104
fruit trees, 140, 145, 147
Fruitful Pimm's, 118

garlic, 107, 119, 128–129
Greek salad, planting for, 100
green (French) beans, 64, 79, 81–82, 98, 145
green tomatoes, 130
greenfly, 148
Greens for wok and health, 133
grow bags, 19

Herb butter, 104
Herbal tea, 73, 115
herbs, 70–73, 104, 115
Homegrown pesto sauce, 104
hoverflies, 63, 146

insecticides, 149

kale, 12, 68–69, 89, 131
Kale and chorizo soup, 69

komatsuna, 125, 133

lamb's lettuce (mâche), 125
land cress, 125
leaf miner, 150
lemon verbena, 73, 115
lemongrass, 109
lemons, 102, 116, 151
lettuce, 8, 37–39, 52, 90, 94, 100, 108,
    124–125, 134, 146
liquid seaweed, 96, 97

mâche (lamb's lettuce), 125
mangetout, 59, 145
manure, 22–24, 30, 31, 40
marigolds, 63, 82
marinades, 115
Mediterranean veggie combos,
    100–101
mibuna, 124, 125, 131, 133
microgreens, 131
mildew
    downy, 39
    powdery, 40, 60, 87, 150
mint, 13, 73, 105, 115, 118, 119, 121
mizuna, 125, 131, 133, 146
mojito cocktails, 73
A mojito to banish a day at the
    office, 118
mustards, 131, 133

nasturtiums, 15, 62, 76, 121, 145, 146
nectarines, 150
nettles, 29, 97
Nicotiana sylvestris, 65, 146

onions, salad, 58, 94
oregano, 71, 100, 101, 115
oriental greens, 94, 122, 146
Oriental larder, 61
oriental salad mixes, 133

pak choi, 61, 94, 109, 133
parsley, 72, 115, 146
pea gravel, 15, 17, 72

pea shoots, 60
peach leaf curl, 150
peaches, 40, 106, 144–145
pears, 140, 142
peas, 59, 60, 64, 80, 94, 98, 131, 145,
    150
peppers, 12, 44, 88–89, 97, 101,
    108–109, 114, 130, 151
perlite, 25, 102
Pesto sauce, 104
plums, 105, 140, 143, 145
pollination, 88, 89, 142
poppies, 15, 65
potato disease, 150
potatoes, 8, 32, 35–36, 60, 69, 112,
    114, 138, 148–149, 150
pumpkins, 50, 88, 133
purslane, 124, 133

Quick, easy, and delicious
    bruschetta, 119

radicchio, 91, 147
radishes, 55, 94
raspberries, 40, 84, 106, 121,
    136–137, 147
raspberry beetle, 135, 137, 151
Ratatouille riot, 101
red mustard, 133
red spider mites, 151
rocket. See arugula
root fly, 61
rosemary, 72, 115
row cover, 36, 124, 134, 147
runner beans, 74, 79–80, 98, 99, 145
rust, 151

sage, 72
salad, 15, 35–39, 58, 94, 125, 133
    A decadent winter salad, 146
    Greek salad, planting for, 100
    Salad herbs, 115
    A salad to put spring in your step,
        60
salad boxes, 52

salad herbs, 115
salad onions (scallions), 58
salad spinners, 38
salsa, 108
scab, common, 150
scale insects, 151
scallions (salad onions), 58, 94
seedling transplants, 13
slugs and snails, 39, 44, 56, 61, 89,
    151
snow peas (mangetout), 59, 145
soil, 21–25
solanum, 65
sorrel, 52, 72, 125, 131
Speedy squash, 132
spinach, 150
squashes, 50, 88, 98, 132–133, 145,
    150
strawberries, 40, 83–86, 97, 146
sugar snap peas, 59–60
sunflowers, 131
sweet corn, 54, 89, 107
sweet peas, 64, 80, 98, 145, 150

tarragon, 13, 71, 104
Thai for two, 109
thyme, 72, 115, 146
tomato feed, 36, 90, 93, 101
tomatoes, 12, 46–47, 77–78, 97, 101,
    108, 115, 130, 145, 148, 151
tools, 13–17
trees, 66–67, 102, 116, 140–141, 147
tulips, 65
tzatziki dip, 119

villains, in gardens, 56–57, 148–151
Viola tricolor (heartsease), 63, 121

watering, 95
white rot, 151
whitefly, 151
window boxes, 20, 56, 76, 101

zucchini, 12, 15, 49, 87, 97, 98, 101,
    145, 150

Resources

Crocus (UK)
www.crocus.co.uk

The first major online plant and gardening equipment supplier and still hard to beat for reliability and range. Their instant herb garden, salad garden, and vegetable garden collections are the ultimate in lazy kitchen gardening and they do a nice line in stylish pots, obelisks, and garden furniture too.

Plantstuff (UK)
www.plantstuff.co.uk

Chic online garden furniture and accessories company. Slate seed labels, bird tables, cloches, olde world wooden seed trays, antique galvanized pots, leather kneelers . . . all the stuff you may not strictly need for your garden, but that you really want all the same.

For the US

Seed Savers Exchange
www.seedsavers.org

Iowa-based nonprofit preserving heirloom and historical varieties of vegetables, fruit, herbs, and flowers. They offer one of the biggest and brightest seed catalogs out there, with tons of organic seeds available as well as transplants. Their website has guides for sowing and saving seeds.

Peaceful Valley Farm & Garden Supply
www.groworganic.com

Huge organic seed and garden tool supplier based in California, with an extensive and super helpful library of how-to videos online. Easy-to-use online ordering.

Johnny's Selected Seed
www.johnnyseeds.com

Employee-owned company based in Maine and one of the original signers of the Safe Seed Pledge, in 1999, to sell only non-GMO (genetically modified organisms) seeds. Huge selection and easy-to-use online ordering.

High Mowing Organic Seeds
www.highmowing.org

One hundred percent organic seed company, New England based, with seeds of all stripes and easy-to-use online ordering.

Johns Hopkins Center for a Livable Future
(Google it)

Comprehensive source of information on urban agriculture and much more.

USDA Land Grant University Website Directory
nifa.usda.gov/land-grant-colleges-and-universities-partner-website-directory

Clickable map connecting you to your state's cooperative extension, the best source of up-to-date gardening advice specific to your area you're likely to find, short of a resident master gardener in your neighborhood.

Duluth Trading Company
www.duluthtrading.com

Plenty of rugged clothing options for men, women, and children, from sun hat to gum boot (Wellington).

Fiskars
www.fiskars.com

Top-of-the-line gardening tools for any task or hand size.

Felco
www.felco.com

Swiss-made gardening gear-maker, famous for their pruners (secateurs) with the grippy red handles.

Acknowledgments

Many thanks to all at Fox Chapel Publishing for giving this little book a new lease of life! Particular thanks to Jeremy Hauck for so thoroughly incorporating my updates. Also to my agent Heather Holden-Brown for her enthusiasm and fun. And as always to Donna and the boys for being excellent, always supportive, and sometimes even eating my vegetables.

Photo Credits

Courtesy of the author: Pages 7 (potted beets), 8 (lettuce and potatoes), 9 (sown pots), 11 (cilantro plant), 36 (chitted potatoes), 37 (lettuce plants), 46 (cherry tomatoes), 68 (green curly kale), 79 (harvested beans), 84 (strawberry blossoms), 88 (green curly kale), 94 (carrot seedlings, seed box), 97 (comfrey), 112 (blue potatoes), 134 (lettuce under cloche), 145 (bottom left: raised bed), and 152 (harvested beets).

Edward Alwrite: Pages 20 (nasturtiums in window box), 27 (beehive compost bins), 39 (leaf lettuce), 44 (peppers), 52 (background: window box), 66 (fig on branch), 70 (potted herbs), 78 (tomatoes up close), 83 (strawberries in box), 90 (background: potted flowers), 93 (blueberries), 106 (raspberries), 135 (blackberries), and 145 (climbers on arbor).

Adrian Clarke Photography: Page 160 (author headshot).

Nila Aye: Illustrations.

iStock: Pages 21 (girl's boots and shovel), 35 (new potatoes), 43 (chard), 53 (carrots), 54 (corn), 55 (radish), 59 (snap peas), 61 (pak choi), 69 (purple kale), 81 (green beans), 92 (artichoke), 126 (fava beans), 129 (garlic bulbs), 132 (pumpkins), and 140 (potted fruit tree).

Shutterstock: kazoka (cover), Hannamariah (pages ii–iii), Zoom Team (pages iv–v), Agenturfotografin (page 12 tomatoes), Andriy Blokhin (12 kale bed), ronstik (12 basil), EvgeniiAnd (12 peppers), Freedom_Studio (13 seed tray), stanga (13 plastic pots), Slaven (13 transplant), Galushko Sergey (14 watering can), Veronika Synenko (14 twine), RTimages (14 garden fork), Sergio Schnitzler (14 spade, 89 corn), TanaCh (14 labels), Danny Smythe (14 trowel, 17 pail), de2marco (14 clay pots), Niik Leuangboriboon (15 Styrofoam), ToeyFatboy (15 broken pot), Marina Lohrbach (16 glazed pot), Jordan Lye (16 fiber cement pot), SomeSense (page16 terracotta pots), De Repente (16 wine crate), Photology1971 (17 tubs), Imfoto (17 boots), Pheobus (17 gravel), Del Boy (18 hanging tomatoes), vm2002 (19 grow bag), Hennadii H (19 tomato illus.), Roman Nerud (20 window box),

Artazum (21 raised beds), Edler von Rabenstein (23 loamy soil), alicja neumiler (23 pitchfork), McGraw (23 chalky soil), Brandon Blinkenberg (25 potting materials), YamabikaY (25 sand), mubus7 (28 leaf cuttings), Madlen (28 vegetable scraps), Sukpaiboonwat (28 coffee grounds), Graham Corney (28 newspaper, 151 rust), nikkytok (28 lawn cuttings), AS Food studio (29 nettle, 63 heartsease), Prapai Butta (29 eggshell), Modgetter (29 food scraps), Lukas Fenzi (29 avocado), xpixel (29 sticks), napocska (30 manure), Bildagentur Zoonar GmbH (31 garden), Anton Khodavoskiy (32 leaf lettuce), vaivirga (33 pots on sill), Sea Wave (32, 34 arugula), corners74 (38 salad spinner), surachet khamsuk (38 seedlings), filippo Giuliani (40 wheel barrow), farbled (41 beets), Vadym Zaitsev (45 pepper), Jewelzz (tomatoes 47, 74), Andrey Shtanko (48, 87 cucumber), Vyaseleva Elena (12, 49 zucchini), MNStudio (50 pumpkins), visivastudio (51 eggplants), r.classen (56 snail),Lisa S. (56, 151, back cover slug), DEJA_VU1990 (57 cat), Grandpa (58 scallions, 150 scab), Peter Turner Photography (60 sweet peas, 80 runner beans, 124 mibuna), Vilor (62, 121 nasturtiums) oksana2010 (62 borage), Kuttelvaserova Stuchelova (63 marigolds, 96 beach), Natalya Bidyukova (63, 121 purple heartsease), Jane McIlroy (64 sweet pea), Oleksandr Kostiuchenko (64 nicotania), Es75 (64 cosmos), Tamara Kulikova (64 poppies), Kyselova Inna (65 dahlia), Mikhail Abramov (65 tulips), Le Do (65 clematis), Matt Gore (65 allium), korkeng (67 fig), KaterinaMatroskin (67 illus.), Olga Miltsova (70 basil), brulove (70 cilantro), Dionisvera (71 oregano, 73 mint), Ines Behrens-Kunkel (71 chives), Valentyn Volkov (71 fennel, 72 sorrel), Nataly Studio (71 tarragon), spline_x (72 thyme), Maks Narodenko (72 parsley), Kaiskynet Studio (72 sage), Superheang168 (72 rosemary), Zuzuan (72 bay), Nikolaeva Galina (73 tea), Scisetti Alfio (73 lemon verbena, 120 borage, 71, 125 chervil), Franz Peter Rudolf (75), fotohunter (77 tomatoes), AVN Photo Lab (85 strawberries), TMsara (91 radicchio), Fotokostic (95 watering), Julia Sudnitskaya (97 nettles), Arina P Habich (98 climber), johnbraid (98 trellis), jonesyinc (98 canes),

Paul Fisher (99 cottage garden), Flower_Garden (99 trellis), Ketrin_Ti (99 arch), hanohiki (100), Ekaterina Pokrovsky (101), Dennis Albert Richardson (103), Magdalena Kucova (104 ice cubes), ILEISH ANNA (104 herb butter), Lesya Dolyuk (104 pesto), Relu1907 (105 plums), Lunov Mykola (105 pruners), JT8 (106 berries), Kajonsak Tui (106 stocking), Maria Komar (108 salsa) Igor Vkv (108 flag), Athi Aachawaradt (109 bird's eye chili), Shane White (109 thai basil), BLUR LIFE 1975 (110, 111), stockcreations (113 corn, 119 bruschetta, 120 salad), Olga Vasilyeva (113 brazier), zi3000 (114), vasanty (115 tea), Lorraine Kourafas (115 pesto), uguruysal (116), Devenorr (117 tea candles), BBA Photography (118, back cover Pimm's), iravgustin (118 background, 121 mojito), Oleksandra Naumenko (119 tzatziki), 5 second Studio (121 ice cubes), eelnosiva (122 fava beans), Hong Vo (122 garlic), abc1234 (122, 124 mizuna), Nika Art (123), Nataliia Pyzhova (124 arugula), Bjoern Wylezich (124 purslane), corners74 (124 lamb's lettuce), kariphoto (125 komatsuna), Premyslaw Muszynski (125 land cress), Manfred Ruckszio (125 French sorrel), webquake (130 tomatoes), diamant24 (130 figs), sarocha wangdee (131 microgreens—top), Kayla Waldorff (131 microgreens—bottom), Diana Taliun (132 squash), Iurii Kachkovskyi (136), Lanav (137), 13Smile (139), wissanustock (141 roots), FooTToo (141 pears), Glushchenko Nataliia (142), hanif66 (143), Daveleephotography.com (144), Del Boy (145 raised beds—right, 146), vincent noel (147 radicchio), Alena Kuzmina (147 frost blankets), Plant Pathology (148 blight), D. Kucharski K. Kucharska (148 black bean aphid, 151 whitefly), Ed Phillips (148 aphid), Susan Law Cain (149 blossom end rot), Floki (149 botrytis), Mangpor_nk (149 caterpillar), Sonsedska Yulia (149 cat), AJCespedes (150 powdery mildew, 151 split tomato), Tamisclao (150 peach leaf curl), Iryna Zhuravel (150 flea beetle), Phakdee kasamsawad (150 leaf miner), Alena Brozova (151 white rot), SIMON SHIM (151 scale), Simone Morris (151 red spider mite), Henrik Larsson (151 raspberry beetle).

About the Author

ALEX MITCHELL is a journalist and gardener who has grown her own fruit and vegetables for almost 20 years. The author of four gardening books including *The Edible Balcony*, *The Rurbanite*, and *Gardening on a Shoestring*, she writes for newspapers and magazines on gardening and outdoor living, with a specialty in making the most of small urban spaces.